1795

Nifty Ninepatches

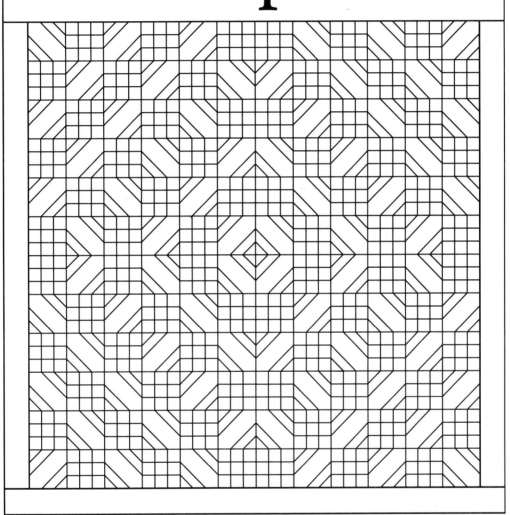

That Patchwork Place®

Carolann M. Palmer

Quilters' Corner
3020 H Street
Sacramento, California 95816
(916) 442-5768

CONTENTS

Dedication

For my granddaughters, whom I hope will follow their mothers, grandmother, and great-grandmother as fourth generation quilters in a few years.

To you, Sara Theres, Rebecca Rose, and Deana Marlaine, this book is dedicated. Happy Quilting!

Acknowledgments

A word of thanks to my husband, Eric, and to my family, who have faithfully supported this project since its inception.

Thanks to the pattern testers, who have generously given of their time and expertise: Liz Thoman, Diane Coombs, Barbara Chesnutt, Judy Pollard, Sue Lopez, Diane Roubal, Nell Moynihan, Cindy Gilbrough, Maggi Zobrist, Ola Bouknight, Bev Bodine, Joyce Miller, Ann Eggers, Sylvia Mittendorf, Sue Anderson, Julie Stewart, Janet Carmichael, and Arlene Sheckler.

Thanks also to Nancy Martin and staff, for their words of encouragement and help.

Credits

Photography . . . . Brian Kaplan
Illustration and Graphics . . . . Karl St. Pierre
Text and Cover Design . . . . Joanne Lauterjung
Editor . . . . Liz McGehee

Nifty Ninepatches©
©1992 by Carolann M. Palmer

That Patchwork Place, Inc.
PO Box 118, Bothell, WA 98041-0118

Printed in the British Crown Colony of Hong Kong
97 96 95 94 93   6 5 4 3 2

Library of Congress Cataloging-in-Publication Data

Palmer, Carolann.
    Nifty ninepatches / Carolann M. Palmer ; photography, Brian Kaplan ; illustration and graphics, Karl St. Pierre ; text and cover design, Joanne Lauterjung ; editor, Liz McGehee.
        p.   cm.
    ISBN 0-943574-95-1 :
        1. Patchwork—Patterns. I. Title
TT835.P353   1992
746.9'7—dc20

91-36166
CIP

No part of this product may be reproduced in any form, unless otherwise stated, in which case reproduction is limited to the use of the purchaser. The written instructions, photographs, designs, projects, and patterns are intended for the personal use of the retail purchaser and are under federal copyright laws; they are not to be reproduced by any electronic, mechanical, or other means, including informational storage or retrieval systems, for commercial use.

The information in this book is presented in good faith, but no warranty is given nor results guaranteed. Since That Patchwork Place, Inc., has no control over choice of materials or procedures, the company assumes no responsibility for the use of this data.

On the front cover: Trellis Garden by Carolann M. Palmer

PREFACE

Some of my earliest memories involve quilts. In my home, a quilt was a Ninepatch. In most cases, it was a Five/Four Ninepatch, which means the corners and center squares were a print, and the other squares were a coordinating solid fabric. Blocks were 9" or 12" and set with sashing. I used to beg my mother to wait until I got home from school to piece her blocks, because then I could sit on the floor behind her sewing machine and cut the block segments almost faster than she could sew. Neighbors came in often to quilt, or we would go to visit. I liked visiting Mrs. Smith, because halfway up the stairway was a special cubbyhole with a doll, cradle, and quilt, and I could sit all by myself and play while the ladies quilted.

My mother used perle cotton and the "gallopy goose" quilting stitch (each stitch about ¼" long) because it was fast. The first "non-Ninepatch" quilt I remember her making was a pieced pink-and-white beauty, where she used regular quilting thread and took small stitches. I asked her why her stitches were so small, and she replied that this was a special quilt.

When my brother came home from the war with a pea coat, the next quilt turned into a sixteen-patch ship. All the ships were navy, the sky was blue, and the sails were many different prints. The quilts I made for my dolls must have been Ninepatches. I know the ones I made for my daughters were.

In recent years, my quilting has progressed far beyond the simple Ninepatch, although they are still my favorites. I have been intrigued with movement across the face of a quilt, achieved by visual texture or the use of textured fabric. "Overs and unders" in woven-look designs are special favorites. The use of two blocks to create another design fascinates me no end!

While I was designing the patterns for the quilts in this book, part of me returned to my childhood, when I would exclaim with glee as a new pattern emerged or a Ninepatch was hidden or disguised.

I hope you will enjoy a serendipitous adventure as you work with these designs. Remember they are only designs. Take them and see what glorious quilts you can make. I guarantee that working with Ninepatches is infectious. Have fun!

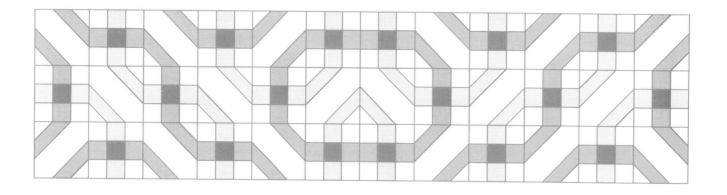

INTRODUCTION

The designs in this book are based on a Ninepatch block alternating with another block to form a new design. Sometimes the Ninepatch is hidden, as in Trellis Garden, Linked Together, or Delipatch. Other places it is merely disguised, as in Hearts Aplenty or Twinkle Twinkle. Sometimes the Ninepatch is hard to hide, as in Star Square or Eternal Chain.

In all cases, the Ninepatch block stands as nine unbroken squares. It may be a Five/Four Ninepatch, where the center and corner squares are a print, or a Four/Five Ninepatch, where the four inner squares are a print. In any case, the color and design are pushed into the next alternate block to make a new design. This book is meant to be a jumping-off point to other designs. The introduction of a third block, as in Bespangled Beauty or Morning Dew, can further change the design, making the design possibilities limitless.

The first part of this book contains basic guidelines to help you have a successful experience. Proper tools, quick techniques, and correct fabric choices are an integral part of this process. For a change, try something different, evaluate it, incorporate it into your quilt if you like it, or toss it out if you don't.

The next section has helpful hints for finishing your own special Ninepatch quilt. The Gallery in full color displays sample quilts and will guide you as you make yours.

The final section contains the patterns for eighteen quilts. Remember, they are only patterns and, hopefully, they will encourage you to make new designs. Templates required for several of the quilts are found on pages 70–71.

Have a great time as you explore the world of Ninepatches!

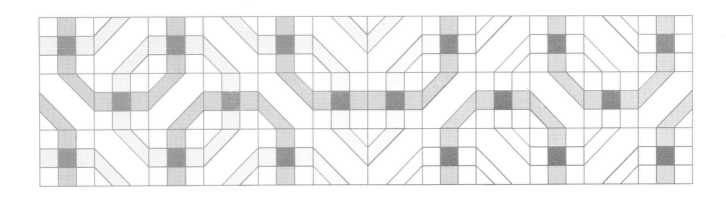

GUIDELINES

Choosing the Design

"I've always wanted to make a quilt. It looks like fun."

"My grandmother made quilts."

"I saw a picture of a quilt that would look nice in my bedroom."

"I went to a quilt show and saw a gorgeous quilt I have to make."

Whatever reason you may have to make a quilt, one of the first places to start is choosing the design. Some questions you may need to ask and answer are: What effect do I want to achieve? Do I want to create movement over the entire surface of the quilt, like Trellis Garden (page 17) or Delipatch (page 30)? What about creating an illusion, like Judy's Window (page 29) or Linked Together (page 27)? Do I want repetitious designs like Shining Path (page 22) or Flypatch (page 24)? Do I want a quilt that lets the viewer see a new design every time they look at it, as in Bespangled Beauty (page 26) and Step by Step (page 21)?

Perhaps you really don't care about all these things. You just want to make a beautiful quilt, with the design chosen because you like it.

Fabric produced today is full of quilt ideas. For instance, Bespangled Beauty started with the iris print, ten months before I knew just what design would be used with it. As I graphed out a possible solution, a star emerged, then it had a shadow. It wasn't until the blocks were sewn and up on my design board that I decided to rotate the Ninepatches ninety degrees. Then I could hardly wait to sew them together.

Take time in this process of quiltmaking to think through what you really want and how you will achieve it. Perhaps the design page will help in this important and fun project.

TO USE THE DESIGN PAGE:

Place tracing paper over the design page. The Ninepatches will show through. On a separate sheet of paper, choose the design you wish from those below and trace about twenty-five times. Cut out these squares.

Now comes the fun part. Lay these squares over the blank squares on the design page. Twist and turn them until you are satisfied with the design. Now, glue the squares to tracing paper and color in the desired colors. You may wish to color in the blocks before arranging.

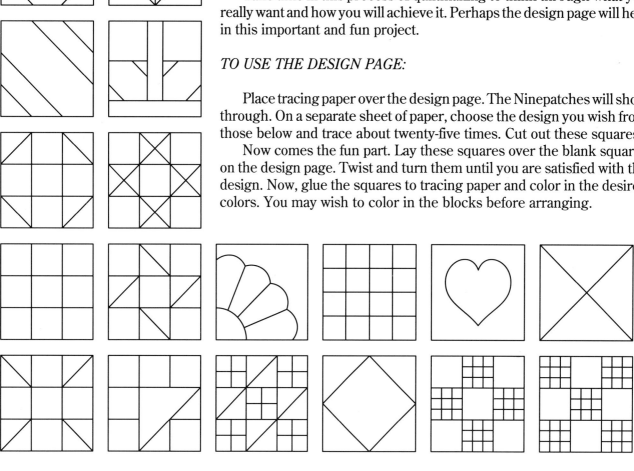

Design Page

Selecting Color and Fabric

When it comes to color selection and choosing fabric, it often boils down to several basic points.

1. Choose one fabric you can't live without, then select fabrics that blend with it.
2. Choose fabrics that give visual texture as well as contrast, or blend with the favorite fabric.
3. Choose a light, medium, and dark from one or two color families.
4. Trust your eye to tell you what you really like.

It's easiest to work with 100 percent cotton fabrics. Be sure to use a variety of large and small prints, stripes, dots, and diagonal print fabrics.

Dark colors recede, and light colors advance, usually. Bright colors excite, and soft colors calm. It is the exceptions to these rules that frustrate or motivate us to action. Background fabric may blend or contrast with other prints, but sometimes a print with a light background does not carry the block pattern very well. Be adventuresome, follow basic color guidelines, then find something with which you can be happy.

Helpful Tools

There are many quilting tools available today that will speed the process of quiltmaking and help in accuracy. The following are a few of the basics.

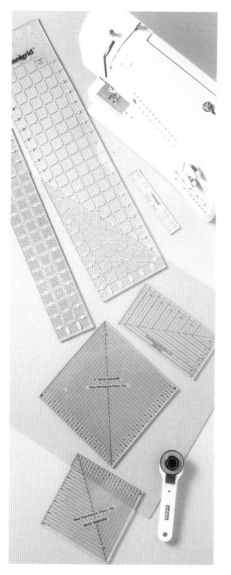

SCISSORS

A pair of fabric scissors is a must. Make sure only fabric is cut with them. Put a padlock on them, if necessary, or hide in a secret place. Paper scissors are also essential for cutting only paper. Keep both sharpened.

ROTARY EQUIPMENT

A rotary cutter, which looks like a pizza cutter, is necessary for accurately cutting quilt pieces. A special self-healing mat and ruler completes this trio of equipment. A variety of sizes is available.

RULERS

Clear acrylic rulers marked in ⅛" increments are essential for rotary cutting. My favorites are the 6" Bias Square® and a 6" x 12" ruler. Other sizes, available at quilt shops, can contribute to a quilter's sanity.

NEEDLES

Use the proper one for each process in quilting. Hand sewing, appliqué, and quilting needles are good starters. A soft-sculpture needle is good when basting your quilt layers together.

PINS

Special quilter's pins are long and essential for pinning together the quilt layers for basting. They are also handy for regular sewing use.

THIMBLE

Thimbles are available in metal, leather, or plastic and come in a variety of shapes and sizes. Find one that fits your finger without easily coming off. Try several and find the style just for you.

MARKERS

There are felt markers, pens, pencils, and chalk in all shapes, colors, and sizes. Make sure that what you get is designed for quilting and test before use to make sure marks are removable.

IRON

A good steam iron is basic, along with a well-padded ironing board. You may want to put padding on a hollow-core door to create a large pressing surface.

SEWING MACHINE

Buy the best you can afford that meets your needs. For basic quilting, you need one with good stitch quality. Have it serviced at least once a year to keep it in good working order.

Getting Started

Once you have chosen your design, purchased your fabric, and have the proper tools, you are ready to begin your quilt. Be sure to preshrink all fabric in a basin of warm water to ensure all dye residue is removed. Rinse until water is clear, then dry fabric and press. This is one step that must be done without fail. Be sure to hand wash, so you can monitor the color of the rinse water.

Accuracy is important in every step of quiltmaking, especially in cutting the fabric, whether cutting strips with the rotary cutter or using templates with scissors. Being off by just 1/16" grows to 1" every 16", which can cause construction problems, especially if the quilt is large.

Rotary-Cutting Techniques

One of the most valuable quilting tools is the rotary cutter. Long strips of fabric cut from selvage to selvage can be cut quickly, accurately, and easily. The strips are then cut into squares and triangles, eliminating the use of templates. Directions for the quilts in this book are written for rotary cutting. If using a rotary cutter for the first time, follow the manufacturer's safety precautions. The following instructions will help you get started. You will need a rotary cutter, self-healing rotary-cutting mat, and a straight-edge rotary ruler, available at your local quilt shop.

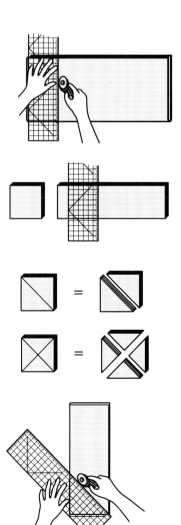

1. Preshrink and press fabric with selvages matching. Fold in half again, lengthwise. You now have four layers.
2. Align straight edge along cross grain of fabric, far enough from the edge to make a clean cut across the width of the fabric. Roll cutter away from you, across the fabric, along the edge of the ruler.
3. Cut fabric into strips, according to the measurement given in the pattern, then cut the strip into squares the width of the strip. Sometimes you will be directed to cut the squares diagonally to create two triangles or to cut twice diagonally to create four triangles.
4. Cut bias strips by aligning the ruler at a 45° angle on the fabric and then cutting. Measure width of strip and make the second cut, parallel to the first.

If the position of the fabric or straight edge is uncomfortable for you, reverse it. You should not feel like a pretzel or have to stand on your head to rotary cut. Practice on some scrap fabric and soon you will have this technique mastered.

Ninepatch Block Construction

In a Ninepatch block, the first set of strips is for the top horizontal row of the block and often, but not always, the bottom row. Therefore, there are usually twice as many. The second set is almost always the middle row, and the color sequence is opposite, in some form, of the first set.

The Ninepatch blocks can easily and quickly be cut and assembled by utilizing the following techniques:

1. Determine fabric color placement. Glue a snippet of fabric to each square on block diagram at top of pattern page to avoid confusion.
2. Cut and sew together three strips (44" long) lengthwise to make one set as indicated by color sequence and directions in each pattern. (Example: "Sew 2 sets purple/light/purple, then cut 32 segments, each 2½" wide.") Press seams of top and bottom rows toward the center strip. Cut into the number of segments indicated in the quilt directions.

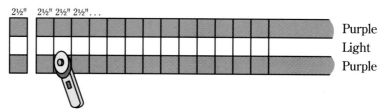

3. Join three strips (44" long) lengthwise to make second set (middle row) as indicated by color sequence and directions in each pattern. (Example: "Sew 1 set light/purple/light, then cut 16 segments, each 2½" wide.") Press seams of middle row away from the center strip. Cut into the number of segments indicated in the quilt directions.

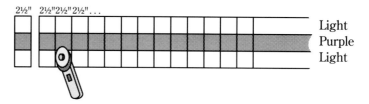

4. Using the block piecing guide at the top of each pattern, sew the segments into groups of three to make the required number of pieced Ninepatch blocks.

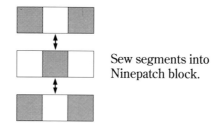

Sew segments into Ninepatch block.

Four Patch Block Construction

Four Patch block construction is similar to Ninepatch construction and varies in the number of strips sewn together.

1. Cut and sew together two strips lengthwise, combining a light strip with a dark strip. (Example: "Sew 6 sets dark/light, then cut 160 segments, each 1½" wide.")

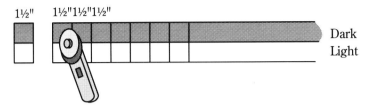

2. Press seams toward the dark strips. Cut into the number of segments indicated in quilt directions.
3. Sew Four Patch blocks.

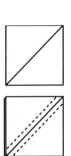

Sew segments into Four Patch block.

Half-Square Triangles

1. Cut squares the size designated in pattern (finished size plus ⅞").
2. Pair two contrasting squares, right sides together.
3. Draw a diagonal line from corner to corner on the wrong side of the lightest square.
4. Stitch ¼" on both sides of line.
5. Cut on the line and press seams to one side of each piece. This makes two half-square triangle units.
6. Square up block to finished size plus ½".

Quarter-Square Triangles

1. Cut squares the size designated in pattern (finished size plus 1¼").
2. Follow steps 2–5 for half-square triangles.
3. Repeat for another set of contrasting squares. Fabric placement is determined by the individual block diagram.
4. Draw a diagonal line from corner to corner on wrong side of one block from each pair just made.
5. Placing blocks right sides together, pin to match in center of block.
6. Sew ¼" on each side of line, then cut on the line and press.
7. Square up block to finished size plus ½".

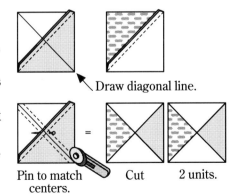

Draw diagonal line.

Pin to match centers.   Cut   2 units.

Trapezoids

1. Cut strip of fabric the width indicated in the individual pattern.
2. Starting at one end of strip, make a 45° cut.

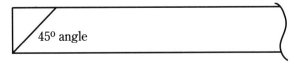

45° angle

3. Measure the long side to the measurement specified in individual quilt pattern. Make another 45° cut in opposite direction.

Continue across strip...

4. Continue across strip, alternating each cut.

Triangles Cut from Strips

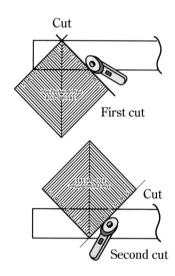

Cut

First cut

Cut

Second cut

1. Cut strip the width indicated in individual pattern.
2. Position Bias Square® with corner at top edge of strip. Bottom edge of strip should be straight across width of ruler.
3. Cut on two sides of Bias Square.
4. Reposition Bias Square with corner at bottom of strip edge and on cutting line. Cut.
5. Continue across strip, alternating each cut.

Quick Geese

1. Cut rectangles and squares the size designated in individual pattern.
2. Draw a line from corner to corner on the back of each square.
3. Position square on one end of rectangle.
4. Sew on the line and trim ¼" away from stitching line.
5. Flip corner up and press.
6. Repeat for other side of rectangle.

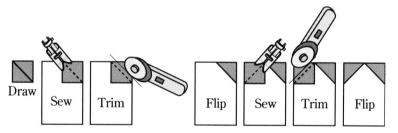

Draw | Sew | Trim | Flip | Sew | Trim | Flip

Note: To utilize the cut-off corner, before trimming in step 4 above, sew another seam ½" from first row of stitching, then cut. You will have a small half-square triangle to use in a doll quilt or potholder.

Paper-Piecing Appliqué

Appliqué is used on two quilts in this book. You may appliqué by hand or machine. I prefer using a technique called paper piecing.

Sew

1. Trace and cut appliquéd pattern pieces from construction paper. Do not add seam allowances.
2. Place paper piece on fabric and pin. Cut, adding a ¼" seam allowance all around as you cut.
3. Fold seam allowance over paper and baste to paper, using a running stitch and sewing through the paper.
4. Clip inner curves and corners as needed.

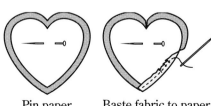

Pin paper to fabric.

Baste fabric to paper, sewing through paper.

5. On outer curves, ease in fullness, using a small running stitch to gather the fabric. Do not sew through paper on outer curves. The basting stitches that go through the paper on either end of the outer curve will hold the fabric to the paper.

6. Baste all fabric pieces to paper. Do not use knots after the last basting stitches, since the basting stitches and paper must be removed in a later step.

7. Press all fabric pieces, making sure that all edges are smooth and free of lumps, bumps, and "points."

8. Appliqué fabric pieces to background, using a small blind stitch and matching thread. Stitches should be about ⅛" apart. When appliqué is completed, turn block to wrong side and carefully cut away background fabric under the appliqué piece, leaving ¼" seam allowance. Remove basting thread, and paper will come out easily. This leaves one less fabric layer to quilt.

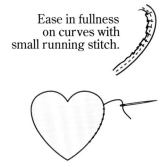

Ease in fullness on curves with small running stitch.

Blindstitch fabric to background.

Sewing

Just as accuracy is important when cutting quilt pieces, it is also vital when sewing the block segments and blocks together. Establish a ¼" seam allowance mark on your sewing machine in some form. Do not assume the line on your throat plate is exactly right. One method is to place masking tape on the throat plate exactly ¼" from the needle. Use three or four layers to make a build-up of tape so the fabric comes to the edge of the tape, or use a piece of adhesive-backed moleskin. You may need to cut out and around the feed dog. It's also helpful to use the built-in even feed or attachment feature on your machine to ensure accuracy. See your machine manual for directions.

Pressing

Always press from the right side of fabric to avoid pleats at the seam line. Press each seam before adding another one that crosses it. When pressing bias edges, be careful not to stretch and distort them. Press seams away from where you will quilt the layers.

For the Ninepatch blocks in this book, press seams in the top and bottom rows toward the center square in each row and press the middle row away from the center square in each row. On the alternate block, if sides are divisible by three like the Ninepatch, reverse the direction, pressing the top and bottom rows away from the center and the middle row toward the center.

When in doubt, look at the quilt top as a whole, then decide how to press. By taking time and planning carefully at this stage of construction, you will eliminate hard bumps within the blocks and at points where the blocks are joined together. And, your seam intersections will be easier to match up.

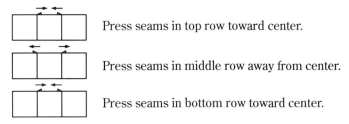

Press seams in top row toward center.

Press seams in middle row away from center.

Press seams in bottom row toward center.

FINISHING YOUR QUILT

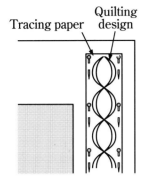

Tracing paper   Quilting design

Mark the Quilt Top

First decide on a quilting design and mark it onto the quilt top. Most of the quilts in this book were quilted by "stitching in the ditch"—in or close to the seam lines. This doesn't require any marking. Some of the quilting designs were marked onto the top with a water-erasable marking pen. I used ¼" masking tape to mark others. Some of the more intricate border designs were machine quilted very quickly by first tracing them onto narrow strips of tracing paper cut the length of each border. I pinned the paper to the border, then stitched with invisible thread, following the quilting design on the paper. The paper tore away easily once the quilting was completed but held up well for quilting a border design with three or four design lines. This method works especially well on dark-colored borders, where it is often difficult to mark quilting lines dark enough to see easily.

Assemble the Layers

Backing   Batting   Quilt top

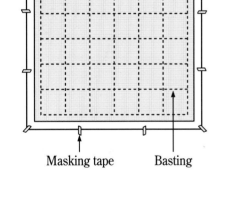

Masking tape   Basting

1. Cut batting and prepare the backing, making them both 2"–4" larger than the finished quilt top all around.
2. With the wrong side up, tape the backing to the floor or a large table, using masking tape and making sure the piece is smooth and taut (free of wrinkles). Place batting on top of backing and smooth out. Carefully place the quilt top, right side up, on batting, making sure the backing and batting extend beyond the top all around. Working from the center out, smooth with hands.
3. Starting at center of quilt, pin all three layers together with quilting pins. Pin at 4"–6" intervals across the quilt surface. Smooth out with hands before adding each pin.
4. Starting at the center and working out, baste quilt layers together in a grid with rows spaced 4"–6" apart over entire quilt surface. Smooth out with hands as needed. Do not trim the excess batting and backing until after binding is attached. If batting is in the way while you quilt, turn the edge of the backing over batting to the front of the quilt and baste in place temporarily.

Quilt

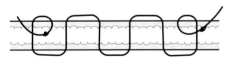

Now you're ready to quilt. I machine quilted most of the quilts in this book with invisible nylon quilting thread. I found this method quick and very practical. I used the even-feed feature on my machine to help feed the fabric through the machine smoothly, eliminating unwanted puckers and pleats on the underside of the quilt. If your machine doesn't have a built-in, even-feed feature, you may be able to purchase an even-feed attachment from your dealer. It's worth checking.

If you prefer to quilt by hand, place your prepared quilt in a hoop or on a quilt frame. To quilt, start at the center and stitch out to the edges, moving the hoop or frame as needed. Using quilting thread and a quilting needle, take tiny running stitches, checking the back of the quilt frequently to be sure the needle goes all the way through the batting and the backing. Remember to quilt around the part of the design you wish

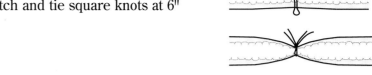

to stand out most to give it an added dimension.

If you prefer to tie your quilt, use embroidery floss, perle cotton, or lightweight yarn. With double thread, stitch and tie square knots at 6" intervals across the surface of the quilt.

Bind

I prefer to use bias binding that I cut and piece from the binding fabric I've chosen.

TO CUT BIAS FOR BINDING:

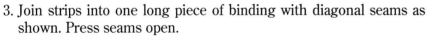

1. Fold the fabric by bringing the selvage edge to meet a straightened edge of the fabric. Press. Cut carefully on the pressed fold. This cut edge is bias.
2. Measure and cut 2½"-wide bias strips parallel to the cut edge.

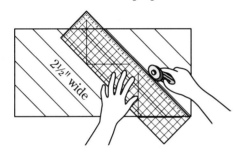

3. Join strips into one long piece of binding with diagonal seams as shown. Press seams open.

Cut strip ends at a 45° angle and seam.

Press seams open.

4. At one end of binding, turn under and press ¼" at a 45° angle as shown. Then fold in half lengthwise, wrong sides together, with raw edges matching. Press lightly.

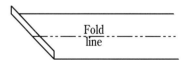

Fold line

TO ATTACH BIAS BINDING:

1. Beginning in the center of one side of the quilt, align the raw edges of the binding with the raw edge of the quilt top.

> **Note:** The batting and backing should still extend beyond the edge of the quilt.

2. Stitch binding to quilt, using a ¼"-wide seam allowance and stopping exactly ¼" from the first corner. Backstitch; remove from machine.

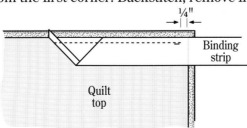

¼"

Binding strip

Quilt top

3. Fold binding away from corner at 90° angle. Finger press the diagonal fold that forms, then carefully flip binding back onto quilt top, forming a fold that is parallel to the edge of the quilt. Begin stitching at edge, backstitching to secure.

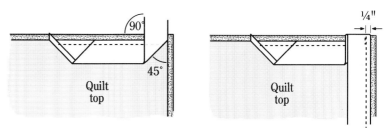

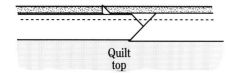

4. Repeat on the remaining three corners. When you reach your starting point, lap the end of the binding over the folded end about 1" and trim away excess binding at a 45° angle. Tuck end into the fold at the beginning of the binding.
5. Trim away the excess batting and backing, leaving a ¼" allowance all around. The excess batting and backing will create a "poof" in the finished binding, making it firm and full. The finished, bound edge will also wear better and longer.
6. Fold binding around batting to back of quilt and slipstitch in place along the seam line. A mitered fold will fall into place at each corner. Stitch in place.

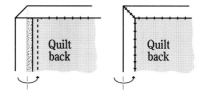

Sleeves and Labels

Take the time to make a sleeve for the back of your quilt so it can be hung. Make a fabric tube almost the width of the finished quilt and hem the ends. Stitch the tube on all sides to the back of your quilt.

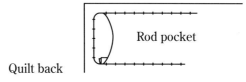

For future generations, be sure to make a label and attach to the back of your quilt. Type on a piece of muslin or embroider, or cross-stitch the name of the quilt, the person who made and quilted it, date completed, owner of quilt, and city and state where it was made. Include any other pertinent information, such as a specific occasion or special fabrics. These labels can be as simple or as fancy as you desire.

Enjoy your beautiful new quilt!

GALLERY

Crossroads by Liz Thoman, 1991, Yakima, Washington, 66" x 66". The Ninepatches leap from the quilt surface as innovative fabric choice, block design, and placement make this Trellis Garden alternative come to life.

Trellis Garden by Carolann M. Palmer, 1990, Seattle, Washington, 66" x 66". The illusion of interlocking rings is achieved by the twisting and turning of both the Ninepatch and the alternate block. Transparency occurs where the two colors meet. Twist and turn several blocks for a new design.

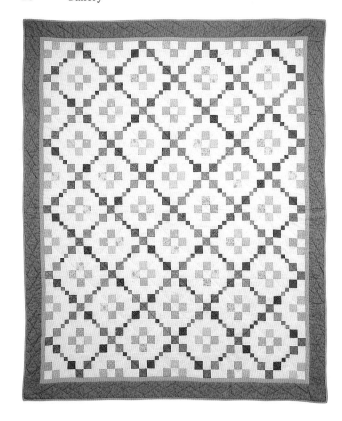

Eternal Chain by Carolann M. Palmer, 1990, Seattle, Washington, 75" x 90". Four Patches work well with the Ninepatches to draw the eye easily from block to block endlessly as the dominate chain lines pull it across the face of this easily pieced beauty.

Honeysuckle Rose by Joyce Miller, 1991, Edmonds, Washington, 88" x 104". Pink roses climb profusely up the trellis in this colorful garden. Their glowing faces peer out, looking for the sunshine. This is a variation of the Eternal Chain design.

Dresden Fans by Ola Bouknight, 1991, Bellingham, Washington, 48" x 48". Fandango in any language means fans of various sizes and colors. The blue fans here are reminiscent of old blue-and-white china plates. The zigzag border calls them to dance.

Fandango by Carolann M. Palmer, 1991, Seattle, Washington, 50" x 50". The special print border surrounds pastel fans dancing in formation amid squares standing all in a row.

Let Your True Colors ... Shine Through by Margaret Zobrist, 1991, Bellevue, Washington, 42" x 42". Each star is made of three shades of one color, giving a colorful glow to the night sky. Twinkle, Twinkle on, little stars.

Twinkle Twinkle by Carolann M. Palmer, 1990, Seattle, Washington, 42" x 42". How I wonder where the Ninepatch is. These stars shine merrily in the dark blue sky, spreading their own kind of joy to earth.

Step by Step by Carolann M. Palmer, 1991, Seattle, Washington, 68" x 68". The Jacob's Ladder block shares space with a Double Ninepatch to create this vivid, flowing stairway to the stars. For an unchained look, play with the blocks before assembly, to create a new design.

Shining Path by Carolann M. Palmer, 1990, Seattle, Washington, 44" x 56". This cheery yellow quilt combines the traditional Snowball block and the Ninepatch. It takes on a three-dimensional look, helped by the addition of a partial block in the border. Where does the road lead?

Iris for Eileen by Judy Pollard, 1991, Seattle, Washington, 45" x 57". The use of a floral motif fabric, framed by the Snowball block, turns the Shining Path pattern into picture frames, creating a gallery of iris prints.

Granny's Posies by Carolann M. Palmer, 1991, Seattle, Washington, 23" x 32". Bright flowers all in a row in Grandma's garden make this a nice quilt on which to record names of your quilt friends, or turn it upside down for a different flower look.

Arbor Rose by Carolann M. Palmer, 1991, Seattle, Washington, 50" x 50". Roses climbing on this arbor peek through the lattice looking for the sun. The light pinwheel stars whirl around, enjoying a bright day.

Water Garden by Nell Moynihan, 1991, Bellingham, Washington, 56" x 67". Shades of sea green create an atmosphere conducive to growing water lilies. The Flypatch pattern is very versatile.

Flypatch by Carolann M. Palmer, 1991, Seattle, Washington, 56" x 68". Christmas prints make this quilt appear seasonal, yet lend vitality for year-round use.

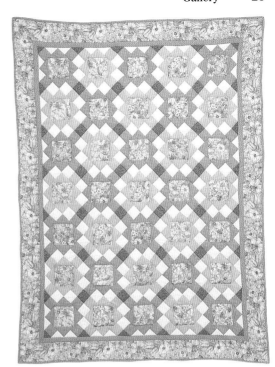

Stacked Tiles by Carolann M. Palmer, 1991, Seattle, Washington, 53" x 69½". Light and dark lattices show depth, while transparency appears where they cross. An almost lacy appearance emerges, while flowers bloom profusely in and around the tiles.

Tossed Salad by Carolann M. Palmer, 1991, Seattle, Washington, 53" x 69". A variation of Stacked Tiles, this almost edible quilt uses a print that lends a festive air as the vegetables are captured inside a red or green square. The Ninepatch blends nicely into the overall design.

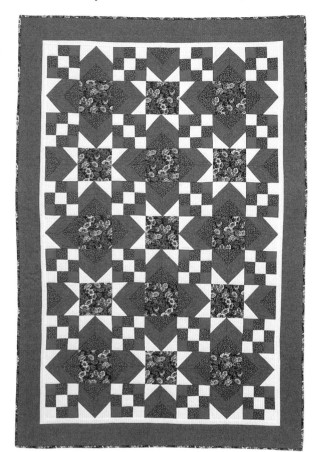

Chevron's Elite by Sue Lopez, 1991, Seattle, Washington, 62" x 84". Brilliant red, white, and blue fabrics provide strong contrast in the stars and Ninepatches to create a different mode from Bespangled Beauty, the original design.

Bespangled Beauty by Carolann M. Palmer, 1990, Seattle, Washington, 52" x 76". A motif print was selected to use with the light star design, while the chevron creates the shadow for it. Look again and another design emerges.

Knot Sew Fast by Arlene Sheckler, 1991, Bothell, Washington, 60" x 60". What has happened to the Ninepatch? It must be tied in with the knots somewhere. This Linked Together design requires a second and third look to see how the chains and Ninepatches are intertwined.

Linked Together by Carolann M. Palmer, 1991, Seattle, Washington, 60" x 60". The mystery of squares linking their arms together will keep your attention on this design. Some link while others just barely touch. This is a great conversation piece.

Star Square by Carolann M. Palmer, 1991, Seattle, Washington, 48" x 60". The use of stripes and large, bold block pieces make this graphic design easy to assemble and enjoy. Can you find the dark stars? How about the light stars?

Hearts Aplenty by Carolann M. Palmer, 1990, Seattle, Washington, 40" x 52". The Ninepatch squares extend the Heart block backgrounds into an intricate, allover pattern. The machine-embroidered ruffle sings out in comfort to all who are under this quilt saying, "I love you."

Judy's Window by Carolann M. Palmer, 1990, Seattle, Washington, 58" x 58". Is it spools, boxes sitting on nothing, a window, or just cubes? You decide, then create your own illusion in your own colors.

Celestial Sparkle by Carolann M. Palmer, 1991, Seattle, Washington, 54" x 54". The Ohio Star block lends itself well to this design as color is uniquely placed, reminiscent of sparkling stars.

Delipatch by Carolann M. Palmer, 1991, Seattle, Washington, 62" x 62". With the help of a few print squares, the Ninepatches twist and turn to make designs on their own. The large, graphic print adds movement and spark.

Under the Sea I by Diane Roubal, 1991, Seattle, Washington, 62" x 62". The colors and fabrics in this vibrant underwater scene appear luminous, creating an eerie feeling. This is a great example of what one Ninepatch with careful color placement can create. The pattern is Delipatch.

Under the Sea II by Diane Roubal, 1991, Seattle, Washington, 62" x 62. Another underwater scene is created from Delipatch. The addition of burgundy to the turquoise makes this design sing.

Morning Dew by Carolann M. Palmer, 1991, Seattle, Washington, 57" x 70". Early morning dew kisses the vivid life-size fruit in this bold quilt and brings to mind a bowl of fruit salad.

QUILT PATTERNS

This section of the book contains directions and patterns for eighteen quilts that have Ninepatch blocks alternating with another block to form an allover design. The finished size of most blocks is 6". Partially shaded line drawings accompany each design. You may use these drawings as a work sheet to plan your own color scheme in the unshaded areas.

The fabrics required for each quilt are based on the original quilt shown in the Gallery (pages 17–32). Fabrics are most often described by color and value (light, medium, dark). You may choose prints or solids in the color and value listed. The variations are endless.

Most of the directions tell you to cut strips of fabric, then cut into squares and cut the squares diagonally to form triangles, when needed in the design. This speed-cutting technique is not only fast but helps make more accurate triangles. Refer to general rotary-cutting techniques on page 9 and specific speed-cutting techniques on pages 10–12. Strips are cut selvage to selvage, and although stated as 44" long, directions have been calculated for a usable 42" fabric width. If, after preshrinking, your fabric is not at least 42" wide, you may need additional yardage for the quilt.

Several quilts require templates. Full-size templates are found on pages 70–71. Each template is identified by the quilt name and a template number or letter. Cutting directions indicate the number of pieces to cut from each fabric. Several templates are labeled "Cut 1 and 1 R," which means to cut a specified number like the template, then flip it over and cut the specified number in reverse. To make it easier, fold fabric wrong sides together and cut only once using the template. This yields one cut like the template and one in reverse.

All templates include a ¼"-wide seam allowance as do the border cutting directions, except where noted. Grain line is noted where needed. Several templates are printed with a fold line. Be sure to make these templates full size before using.

Borders are straight-sewn. If mitered corners are desired, or striped fabric is used in borders, adjust yardage and cutting directions.

Directions for pinning, basting, quilting, and binding your quilt are given on pages 14–16.

TRELLIS GARDEN

Color Photo: page 17
Quilt Size: 66" x 66"
Block Size: 4½"
Templates: page 70

Materials: (44"-wide fabric)
2½ yds. light print (L)
1 yd. purple (P)
⅓ yd. blue-purple (B/P)
2¼ yds. blue (B)
4 yds. backing
1 yd. binding
70" x 70" quilt batting

Block A

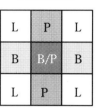

Make 72

Block B

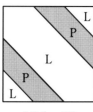

Make 36

Block C

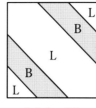

Make 36

CUTTING: All strips are cut cross grain.

From the light print, cut:
16 strips, each 2" wide;
8 strips, each 5" wide, then cut 72 of Trellis Garden Template 1 from the strips;
6 strips, each 2½" wide. Then cut 72 squares, each 2½" x 2½". Cut squares once diagonally to make 144 triangles.

From the purple, cut:
8 strips, each 2" wide;
4 strips, each 4" wide, then cut 72 of Trellis Garden Template 2.

From the blue-purple, cut:
4 strips, each 2" wide.

From the blue, cut:
8 strips, each 2" wide;
4 strips, each 4" wide, then cut 72 of Trellis Garden Template 2;
6 strips, each 6½" wide. Join short ends to make one long strip, then cut 2 pieces, each 54½" long, for side borders and 2 pieces, each 66½" long, for top and bottom borders.

DIRECTIONS

1. Block A: Make 72 blocks. Use 2"-wide strips. Following directions for Ninepatch block construction on page 10, sew:
   ☐ 8 sets of light print/purple/light print, then cut into 144 segments, each 2" wide;
   ☐ 4 sets of blue/blue-purple/blue, then cut into 72 segments, each 2" wide. Piece strips into Ninepatch blocks.
2. Block B: Make 36 blocks. Sew together as in diagram above, using light-print triangles, Template 1 pieces, and purple Template 2 pieces.
3. Block C: Make 36 blocks. Sew together as for Block B, using light-print triangles, Template 1 pieces, and blue Template 2 pieces.
4. Following quilt piecing guide on opposite page, piece blocks into rows, then join rows. Sew borders to sides, then to top and bottom.
5. Pin, baste, quilt, and bind, following directions on pages 14–16.

Note: Carefully pin sides of blocks together where diagonal lines meet straight lines so seams match after stitching.

GRANNY'S POSIES

Color Photo: page 23
Quilt Size: 23" x 32"
Block Size: 3"

Block A

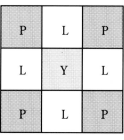

Block B

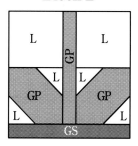

Make 20   Make 20

Materials: (44"-wide fabric)
½ yd. light (L)
⅛ yd. yellow solid or print (Y)
⅛ yd. each of 4 floral prints (P)
⅛ yd. green solid (GS)
¼ yd. green print (GP)
⅛ yd. inner border
½ yd. outer border
¾ yd. backing
½ yd. binding
27" x 36" quilt batting

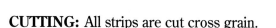

CUTTING: All strips are cut cross grain.

From the light, cut:
3 strips, each 1½" wide; cut each strip into 2 equal lengths;
2 strips, each 1½" wide;
2 strips, each 1¾" wide; cut into 40 squares, each 1¾" x 1¾";
3 strips, each 1⅛" wide; cut into 80 squares, each 1⅛" x 1⅛".

From the yellow, cut:
1 strip, 1½" wide.

From each floral print, cut:
1 strip, 1½" wide; cut into 2 equal lengths.

From the green solid, cut:
2 strips, each 1" wide; cut into 20 segments, each 3½" long.

From the green print, cut:
2 strips, each 1" wide; cut into 20 segments, each 3" long;
2 strips, each 1¾" wide; cut into 40 squares, each 1¾" x 1¾".

From the inner border fabric, cut:
2 strips, each 1½" wide. From each strip, cut 1 piece, 24½" long, for side borders and 1 piece, 17½" long, for top and bottom borders.

From the outer border fabric, cut:
4 strips, each 3½" wide. From these strips, cut 2 pieces, each 26½" long, for side borders and 2 pieces, each 23½" long, for top and bottom borders.

DIRECTIONS

1. Block A: Make 20 blocks. Use 1½"-wide strips. Following directions for Ninepatch block construction on page 10, make 5 blocks with each of the 4 prints. Sew:
   ☐ 1 set of print/light/print, then cut into 10 segments, each 1½" wide;
   ☐ 1 set of light/yellow/light, then cut into 20 segments, each 1½" wide. Piece into Ninepatch blocks.
2. Block B: Make 20 blocks. Following the quick-geese method on page 12, position and sew 1⅛" light squares over opposite corners of 1¾" green print squares as shown in diagram.

Piece block as shown in diagram.

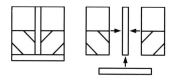

3. Following quilt piecing guide below, piece blocks into rows, then join rows to complete quilt top. Sew borders to sides, then to top and bottom.

4. Pin, baste, quilt, and bind, following directions on pages 14–16.

Note: Don't hesitate to try the quick-geese method on the leaves. It saves a lot of time and makes this quilt a breeze to stitch.

JUDY'S WINDOW

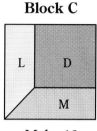

Color Photo: page 29
Quilt Size: 58" x 58"
Block Size: 6"

Block A
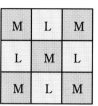

M	L	M
L	M	L
M	L	M

Make 32

Block B

D	L
M	

Make 16

Block C

L	D
	M

Make 16

Materials: (44"-wide fabric)
1 yd. light (L)
1½ yds. total of various mediums (M)
⅔ yd. dark (D)
¼ yd. inner border
1 yd. outer border
3½ yds. backing
1 yd. binding
62" x 62" quilt batting

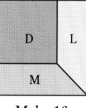

CUTTING: All strips are cut cross grain.

From the light, cut:
6 strips, each 2½" wide; cut into 32 segments, each 6½" long;
8 strips, each 2½" wide; cut each strip into 2 equal lengths.

From the mediums, cut:
6 strips, each 2½" wide; cut into 32 segments, each 6½" long;
10 strips, each 2½" wide; cut each strip into 2 equal lengths.

From the dark, cut:
4 strips, each 4½" wide; cut into 32 squares, each 4½" x 4½".

From the inner border fabric, cut:
5 strips, each 1½" wide. Join short ends to make one long strip, then cut 2 pieces, each 48½" long, for sides and 2 pieces, each 50½" long, for top and bottom borders.

From the outer border fabric, cut:
6 strips, each 4½" wide. Join short ends to make one long strip, then cut 2 pieces, each 50½" long, for side borders and 2 pieces, each 58½" long, for top and bottom borders.

DIRECTIONS

1. Block A: Make 32 blocks. Use 2½"-wide half strips. Following directions for Ninepatch block construction on page 10, sew:
   □ 8 sets of medium/light/medium, then cut 64 segments, each 2½" wide;
   □ 4 sets of light/medium/light, then cut 32 segments, each 2½" wide.
   Piece into Ninepatch blocks.
2. Block B: Make 16 blocks. Use 2½"-wide strips. Sew:
   □ 6½" light segment to right side of dark 4½" square, ending stitching ¼" from bottom edge of square;
   □ 6½" medium segment to bottom of square, starting at outside edge and ending seam in same stitch as first seam. Starting at outside edge in right corner, sew at a 45° angle and end seam in same stitch as previous two seams. Backstitch. Trim seam to ¼" and press.

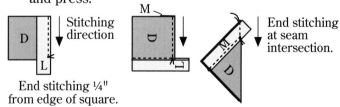

Square up block to 6½".
3. Block C: Make 16 blocks. Piece like Block B but with the light on the left side of the dark square.

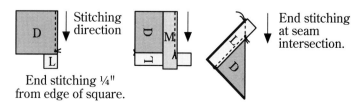

4. Following quilt piecing guide below, piece blocks into rows, then join rows. Sew borders to sides, then to top and bottom.

5. Pin, baste, quilt, and bind, following directions on pages 14–16.

Note: Changing the arrangement of blocks can make this quilt into a variety of imaginative designs. Try using several different colors, arranged by color group.

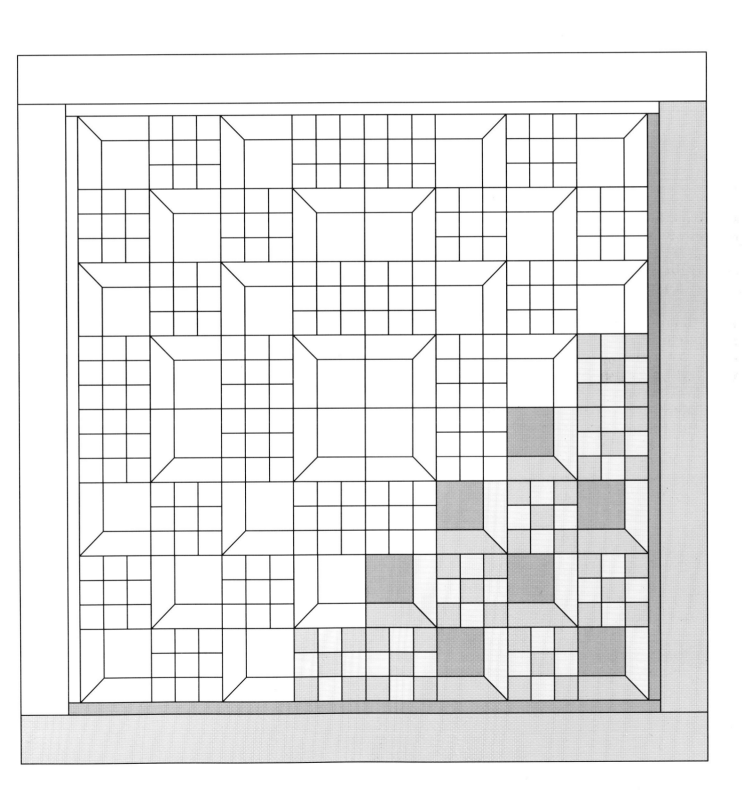

SHINING PATH

Color Photo: page 22
Quilt Size: 44" x 56"
Block size: 6 "

Materials: (44"-wide fabric)
2 yds. light (L)
1½ yds. various yellows (Y)
¼ yd. inner border
¾ yd. outer border
3 yds. backing
½ yd. binding
48" x 60" quilt batting

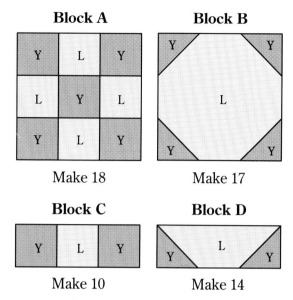

Block A
Make 18

Block B
Make 17

Block C
Make 10

Block D
Make 14

CUTTING: All strips are cut cross grain.

From the light, cut:
9 strips, each 2½ wide. From 3 of these strips, cut a total of 14 segments, each 6½" long. Cut each of the remaining strips into 2 equal lengths;
6 strips, each 6½" wide. From these strips, cut 17 squares, each 6½" x 6½".

From the yellows, cut:
12 strips, each 2½" wide. Cut each strip into 2 equal lengths;
7 strips, each 2½" wide. From these strips, cut 96 squares, each 2½ " x 2½";
4 squares, each 2½" x 2½".

From the inner border fabric, cut:
4 strips, each 1½" wide. Join short ends to make one long strip. Cut 2 pieces, each 46½" long, for side borders and 2 pieces, each 36½" long, for top and bottom borders.

From the outer border fabric, cut:
5 strips, each 5" long. Join short ends to make one long strip. Cut 2 pieces, each 48½" long, for side borders and 2 pieces, each 46½" long, for top and bottom borders.

DIRECTIONS

1. Block A: Make 18 blocks. Use 2½"-wide strips. Following directions for Ninepatch block construction on page 10, sew:
   □ 6 sets yellow/light/yellow, then cut 46 segments, each 2½" wide. Reserve 10 segments for Block C. Cut 5 light and 5 yellow 2½"-wide strips in half crosswise.
   □ 5 sets light/yellow/light. Cut 18 segments, each 2½" wide. Piece into Ninepatch blocks.
2. Block B: Make 17 blocks. Following the quick-geese method on page 12, position and sew yellow 2½" squares in each of 4 corners of 17 light 6½" squares. Use remaining squares in step 4 (Block D).
3. Block C: Use the 10 segments reserved from step 1, Block A.
4. Block D: Make 14 blocks. Following diagram above and using the quick-geese method on page 12, sew remaining yellow squares from step 2 to the short ends of the 14 light rectangles.
5. Following quilt piecing guide on opposite page, piece blocks into rows, then join rows. Sew borders to sides, then to top and bottom.
6. Pin, baste, quilt, and bind, following directions on pages 14–16.

Note: To maintain crispness of design, match seams carefully. When a diagonal seam meets a straight seam, a precise seam allowance and careful pinning is required.

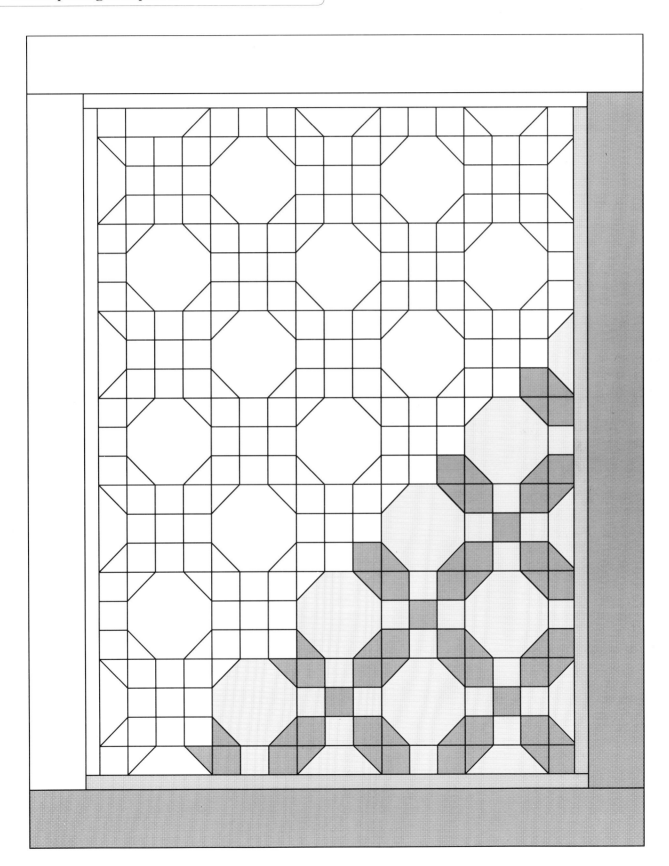

BESPANGLED BEAUTY

Color Photo: page 26
Quilt Size: 52" x 76"
Block size: 6"
Template: page 71

Materials: (44"-wide fabric)
1 yd. light (L)
1 yd. medium (M)
⅓ yd. dark (D)
1 yd. dark print (DP)
⅔ yd. light print (LP)
⅓ yd. inner border
1 yd. outer border
4⅓ yds. backing
½ yd. binding
56" x 80" quilt batting

Block A

Make 24

Block B

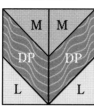

Make 38

Block C

Make 15

CUTTING: All strips are cut cross grain.

From the light, cut:
5 strips, each 2½" wide;
3 strips, each 3⅞" wide. Cut 38 squares, each 3⅞" x 3⅞", then cut once diagonally to make 76 triangles.

From the medium, cut:
7 strips, each 2½" wide;
4 strips, each 3⅞" wide. Cut 38 squares, each 3⅞" x 3⅞", then cut once diagonally to make 76 triangles.

From the dark, cut:
3 strips, each 2½" wide.

From the dark print, cut:
9 strips, each 3½" wide. Using the Bespangled Beauty Template on page 71, cut 38 and 38 reversed.

From the light print, cut:
3 strips, each 6½" wide. Cut 15 squares, each 6½" x 6½". Use these for Block C.

From the inner border fabric, cut:
6 strips, each 1½" wide. Join short ends to make one long strip, then cut 2 pieces, each 66½" long, for side borders and 2 pieces, each 44½" long, for top and bottom borders.

From the outer border fabric, cut:
6 strips, each 4½" wide. Join short ends to make one long strip, then cut 2 pieces, each 68½" long, for side borders and 2 pieces, each 52½" long, for top and bottom borders.

DIRECTIONS

1. Block A: Make 24 blocks. Use 2½"-wide strips. Following directions for Ninepatch block construction on page 10, sew:
   □ 3 sets dark/medium/light. Cut 48 segments, each 2½" wide.
   □ 2 sets medium/light/medium. Cut 24 segments, each 2½" wide. Piece into Ninepatch blocks.
2. Block B: Make 38 blocks. Following diagram, sew light and medium triangles to dark print pieces. Take care in placement of reverse pieces. For easy piecing, press seams on left half of block toward the bottom, and on the right half of block, toward the top, before joining the two halves to form the completed block.

Press seams toward bottom.   Press seams toward top.

3. Carefully following quilt piecing guide on opposite page, piece blocks into rows, then join rows. Sew borders to sides, then to top and bottom.
4. Pin, baste, quilt, and bind, following directions on pages 14–16.

Note: When piecing Block B, carefully align the triangles to the chevron pieces so they will be straight when sewn, then pressed.

DELIPATCH

Color Photo: page 30
Quilt Size: 62" x 62"
Block Size: 6"

Block A

M1	L	L
D	M1	L
M2	D	M1

Make 52

Block B

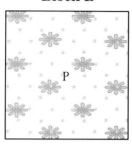

P

Make 12

Materials; (44"-wide fabric)
1 yd. light (L)
1 yd. first medium (M1)
⅓ yd. second medium (M2)
⅔ yd. dark (D)
½ yd. bold, graphic print (P)
¼ yd. inner border
1¼ yds. outer border
3½ yds. backing
1 yd. binding
66" x 66" quilt batting

CUTTING: All strips are cut cross grain.

From the light, cut:
12 strips, each 2½" wide.

From the first medium, cut:
12 strips, each 2½" wide.

From the second medium, cut:
4 strips, each 2½" wide.

From the dark, cut:
8 strips, each 2½" wide.

From the print, cut:
2 strips, each 6½"wide. Cut 12 squares, each 6½" x 6½". Use these for Block B.

From the inner border fabric, cut:
5 strips, each 1½" wide. Join short ends to make one long strip, then cut 2 pieces, each 48½" long, for side borders and 2 pieces, each 50½" long, for top and bottom borders.

From the outer border fabric, cut:
6 strips, each 6½" wide. Join short ends to make one long strip, then cut 2 pieces, each 50½" long, for side borders and 2 pieces, each 62½" long, for top and bottom borders.

DIRECTIONS

1. Block A: Make 52 blocks. Use 2½"-wide strips. Following directions for Ninepatch block construction on page 10, sew:
   - ☐ 4 sets first medium/light/light, then cut 52 segments, each 2½" wide;
   - ☐ 4 sets dark/first medium/light, then cut 52 segments, each 2½" wide;
   - ☐ 4 sets second medium/dark/first medium, then cut 52 segments, each 2½" wide.
   Piece into Ninepatch blocks.
2. Following quilt piecing guide on opposite page, piece blocks into rows, then join rows. Sew borders to sides, then to top and bottom.
3. Pin, baste, quilt, and bind, following directions on pages 14–16.

Note: After laying out the blocks in your own design, take care to sew in rows, or you may have an unplanned twist when piecing is finished.

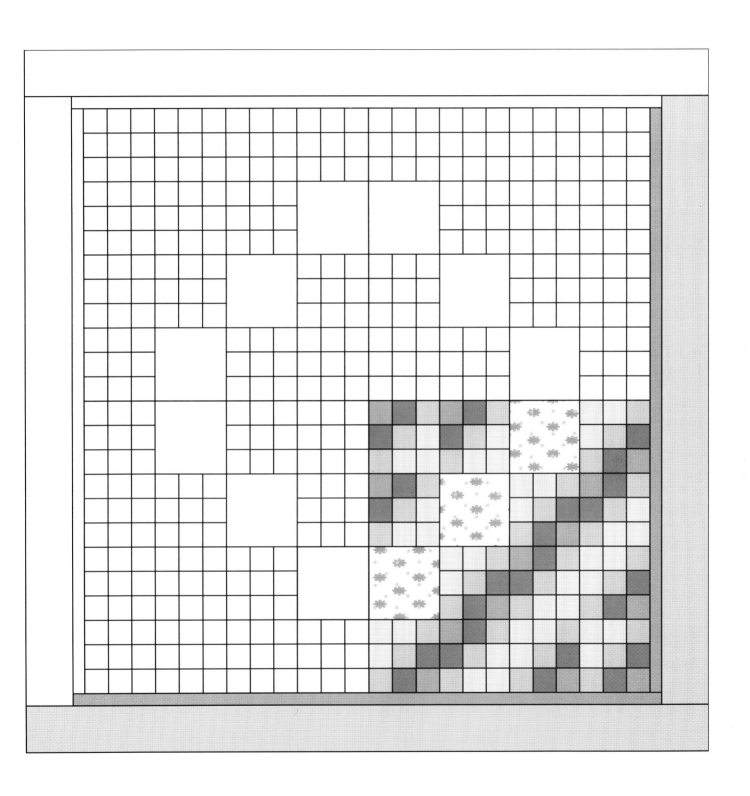

FLYPATCH

Color Photo: page 24
Quilt Size: 56" x 68"
Block Size: 6"

Materials: (44"-wide fabric)
1 yd. red print (RP)
1 yd. red solid (R)
1 yd. light (L)
1 yd. small print (SP)
1 yd. green solid or print(G)
⅓ yd. inner border
1 yd. outer border
4 yds. backing
1 yd. binding
60" x 72" quilt batting

Block A

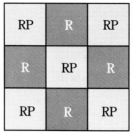

Make 32

Block B

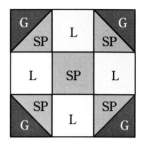

Make 32

Block C

Make 14

Block D

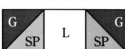

Make 18

CUTTING: All strips are cut cross grain.

From the red print, cut:
12 strips, each 2½" wide;
4 squares, each 2½" x 2½", for corners.

From the red solid, cut:
9 strips, each 2½" wide.

From the light, cut:
10 strips, each 2½" wide. Cut 6 strips into 82 squares, each 2½" x 2½".

From the small print, cut:
2 strips, each 2½" wide; ·
7 strips, each 2⅞" wide. Cut 82 squares, each 2⅞" x 2⅞".

From the green, cut:
7 strips, each 2⅞" wide. Cut 82 squares, each 2⅞" x 2⅞".

From the inner border fabric, cut:
6 strips, each 1½" wide. Join short ends to make one long strip, then cut 2 pieces, each 58½" long, for side borders and 2 pieces, each 48½" long, for top and bottom borders.

From the outer border fabric, cut:
6 strips, each 4½" wide. Join short ends to make one long strip, then cut 2 pieces, each 60½" long, for side borders and 2 pieces, each 56½" long, for top and bottom borders.

DIRECTIONS

1. Block A: Make 32 blocks. Use 2½"-wide strips. Following directions for Ninepatch block construction on page 10, sew:
   □ 5 sets red print/red solid/red print, then cut 78 segments, each 2½" wide;
   □ 2 sets red solid/red print/red solid, then cut 32 segments, each 2½" wide.
   Piece into Ninepatch blocks. Use remaining 14 segments for Block C.
2. Block B: Make 32 blocks. Use 2½"-wide strips. Following directions for half-square triangles on page 11, pair 2⅞" small print squares and 2⅞" green squares, then sew. Square up the resulting 164 blocks to 2½" squares. Sew these squares to light squares for 64 top and bottom rows and 18 Block D. Sew 2 sets of light/small print/light, then cut 32 segments, each 2½" wide. Sew pieced segments together to make Block B.
3. Following quilt piecing guide on opposite page, alternate and sew Blocks A and B into rows. Add Blocks C and D to the ends of each completed row, referring to piecing guide for correct placement.

Join rows into quilt top. Piece remaining C and D blocks into 2 strips with a red-print corner block at each end. Sew to top and bottom edges of quilt top.

5. Pin, baste, quilt, and bind, following directions on pages 14–16.

Note: Take your time when selecting fabric for this quilt. You will be rewarded for it. Think about how you want the chains and stars to appear before you make your final selections.

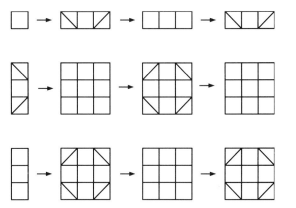

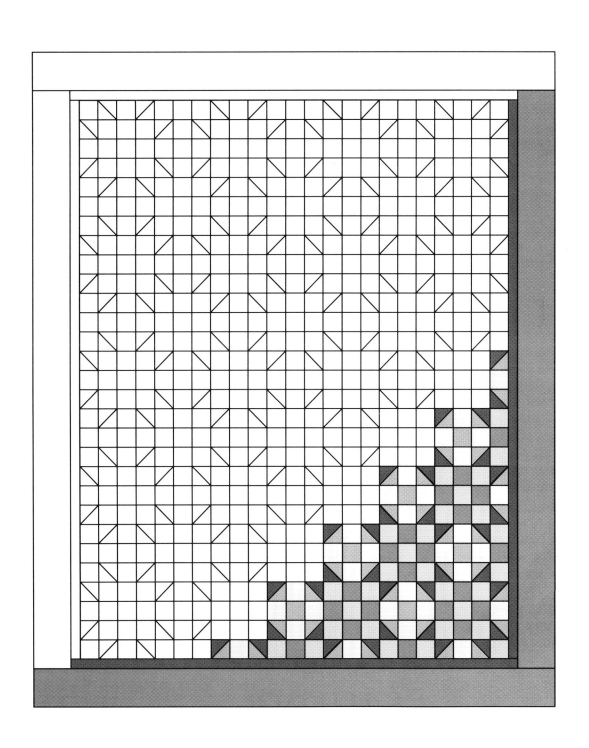

CELESTIAL SPARKLE

Color Photo: page 29
Quilt Size: 54" x 54"
Block Size: 6"
Templates: page 71

Materials: (44"-wide fabric)
1¼ yds. dark purple (D)
1 yd. medium purple (M)
1¼ yds. light (L)
¼ yd. medium turquoise (T)
¼ yd. middle border
⅔ yd. outer border
3¼ yds. backing
1 yd. binding
58" x 58" quilt batting

Block A

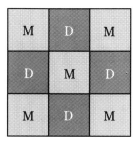

Make 25

Block B

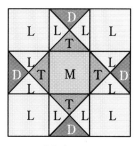

Make 24

CUTTING: All strips are cut cross grain.

From the dark purple, cut:
10 strips, each 2½ wide;
2 strips, each 3¼" wide. Cut into 24 squares, each 3¼" x 3¼";
4 squares, each 3¼" x 3¼". Cut twice diagonally to make 16 triangles for inner border.

From the medium purple, cut:
10 strips, each 2½" wide. Cut 2 strips into 24 squares, each 2½" x 2½".

From the light, cut:
6 strips, each 2½" wide. Cut into 96 squares, each 2½" x 2½";
4 strips, each 3¼" wide. Cut into 48 squares, each 3¼" x 3¼";
5 strips, each 1½" wide. Cut 12 of Celestial Sparkle Template 1; cut 2 plus 2 reversed each of Celestial Sparkle Templates 2 and 3 for inner border.

From the medium turquoise, cut:
2 strips, each 3¼" wide. Cut into 24 squares, each 3¼" x 3¼".

From the middle border fabric, cut:
5 strips, each 1½" wide. Join short ends to make one long strip, then cut 2 pieces, each 44½" long, for side borders and 2 pieces, each 46½" long, for top and bottom borders.

From the outer border fabric, cut:
5 strips, each 3½" wide. Join short ends to make one long strip, then cut 2 pieces, each 46½" long, for side borders and 2 pieces, each 53½" long, for top and bottom borders.

DIRECTIONS

1. Block A: Make 25 blocks. Use 2½"-wide strips. Following directions for Ninepatch block construction on page 10, sew:
   □ 4 sets of medium purple/dark purple/medium purple, then cut 50 segments, each 2½" wide;
   □ 2 sets of dark purple/medium purple/dark purple, then cut 25 segments, each 2½" wide.
   Piece into Ninepatch blocks.
2. Block B: Make 24 blocks. Following directions for quarter-square triangles on page 11, use the 3¼" squares of light, dark purple, and medium turquoise to sew 96 units.

Piece Block B using these units and light and medium-purple squares as shown in diagram above.
3. Following quilt piecing guide on opposite page, piece blocks into rows, then join rows. Piece the inner border sides, then the top and bottom, using light A, B, and C pieces and dark triangles. Sew inner bor-

ders to sides of quilt, then to top and bottom edges.
Repeat with middle and then outer borders.

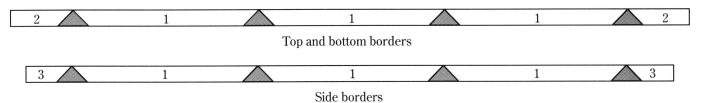

Top and bottom borders

Side borders

4. Pin, baste, quilt, and bind, following directions on
   pages 14–16.

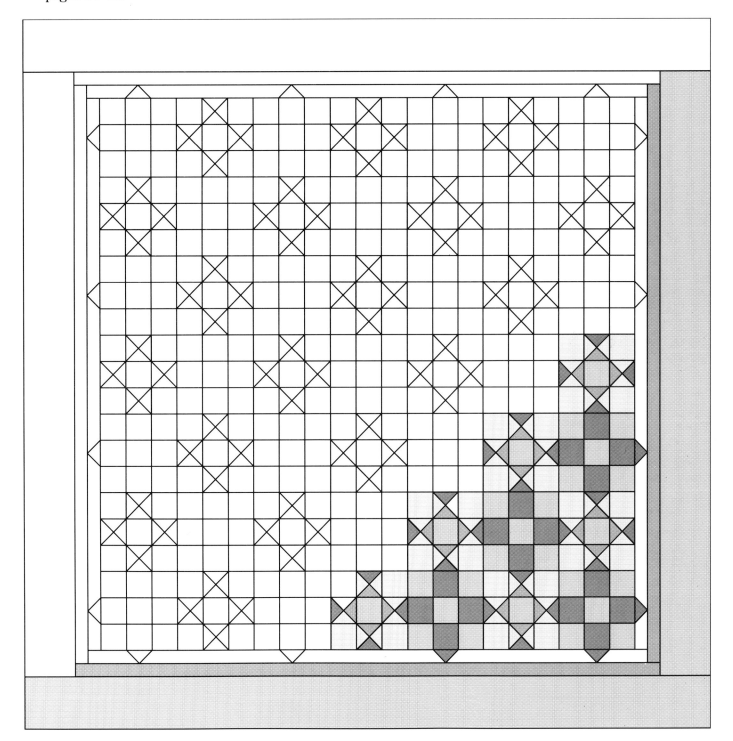

TWINKLE TWINKLE

Color Photo: page 20
Quilt Size: 42" x 42"
Block Size: 6"

Materials: (44"-wide fabric)
1½ yds. navy for background and outer border (N)
⅔ yd. total of various yellows (Y)
¼ yd. inner border
1½ yds. backing
½ yd. binding
46" x 46" quilt batting

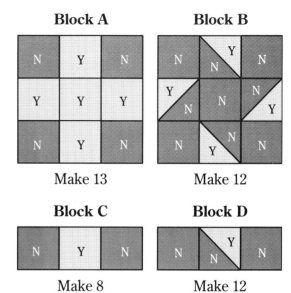

Block A
Make 13

Block B
Make 12

Block C
Make 8

Block D
Make 12

CUTTING: All strips are cut cross grain.

From the navy, cut:
10 strips, each 2½" wide. Cut into 156 squares, each 2½" x 2½";
2 strips, each 2⅞" wide. Cut into 30 squares, each 2⅞" x 2⅞";
4 strips, each 3½" wide. Cut 2 pieces, each 36½" long, for side borders and 2 pieces, each 42½" long, for top and bottom borders.

From the yellows, cut:
5 strips, each 2½" wide. Cut into 73 squares, each 2½" x 2½";
2 strips, each 2⅞" wide. Cut into 30 squares, each 2⅞" x 2⅞".

From the inner border fabric, cut:
4 strips, each 1½" wide. Cut 2 pieces, each 34½" long, for side borders and 2 pieces, each 36½" long, for top and bottom borders.

DIRECTIONS

1. Block A: Make 13 blocks. Use 2½" squares. Piece yellow and navy squares into 3 rows with 3 squares in each row as shown in diagram.
2. Block B: Make 12 blocks. Follow directions for making half-square triangles on page 11. Use 30 yellow and 30 navy squares, each 2⅞" x 2⅞". This makes 60 half-square triangle units. Combine with navy squares for Block B.
3. Sew Blocks C and D as shown in diagrams above.
4. Following quilt piecing guide on opposite page, piece blocks into rows, then join rows, using the 4 remaining navy squares for the corners. Sew inner borders to sides, then to top and bottom. Repeat with outer borders.
5. Pin, baste, quilt, and bind, following directions on pages 14–16.

Note: This quilt is not speed-cut or pieced because of the significant use of randomly placed squares of one color. If you are accustomed to assembling quilts with the speed methods, you may find this method of block placement to be a delightful change of pace. I appreciate the speed methods and generally use them as much as possible, but this quilt was especially enjoyable to put together using the method described above. Careful alignment of contrasting blocks will make this quilt really twinkle, especially if your fabrics are high-contrast colors.

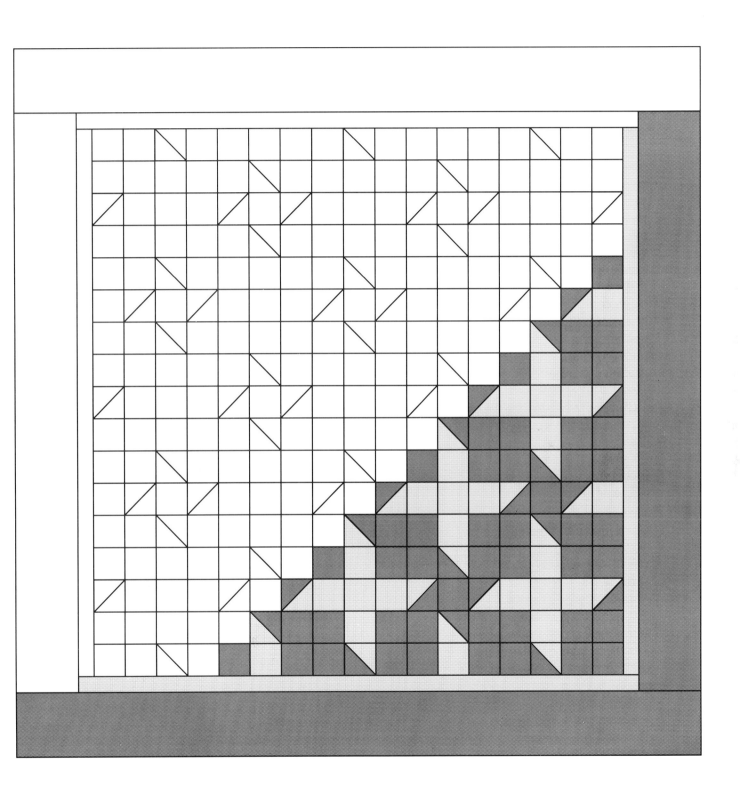

FANDANGO

Color Photo: page 19
Quilt Size: 50" x 50"
Block size: 6"
Templates: page 71

Materials: (44"-wide fabric)
  1¼ yds. light (L)
  ¼ yd. medium (M)
  ¼ yd. dark (D)
  ¼ yd. medium for fan centers (MF)
  ⅛ yd. each of 4 prints (P)
  ¼ yd. inner border
  1 yd. outer border
  3 yds. backing
  ½ yd. binding
  54" x 54" quilt batting

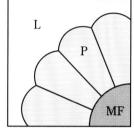

Block A

D	L	M
L	M	L
M	L	D

Make 16

Block B

L
P
MF

Make 20

CUTTING: All strips are cut cross grain.

From the light, cut:
4 strips, each 6½" wide. Cut into 20 squares, each
  6½" x 6½";
4 strips, each 2½" wide.

From the medium, cut:
3 strips, each 2½" wide.

From the dark, cut:
2 strips, each 2½" wide.

From the medium fabric for fan centers, cut:
2 strips, each 3" wide. Cut 20 of Fandango
  Template 2.

From each of the 4 prints, cut:
20 of Fandango Template 1, adding ¼" seam
  allowance.

From the inner border fabric, cut:
4 strips, each 1½" wide. Join short ends to make one
  long strip, then cut 2 pieces, each 36½" long, for
  side borders and 2 pieces, each 38½" long, for top
  and bottom borders.

From the outer border fabric, cut:
5 strips, each 6½" wide. Join short ends to make one
  long strip, then cut 2 pieces, each 38½" long, for
  side borders and 2 pieces, each 50½" long, for top
  and bottom borders.

DIRECTIONS

1. Block A: Make 16 blocks. Use 2½"-wide strips.
   Following directions for Ninepatch block construction on page 10, sew:
   - ☐ 2 sets medium/light/dark, then cut 32 segments,
     each 2½" wide;
   - ☐ 1 set light/medium/light, then cut 16 segments,
     each 2½" wide.
     Piece into Ninepatch blocks.
2. Block B: Make 20 blocks. Paper-piece 80 fan segments (Template 1), following the directions on
   pages 12–13. Sew into units of 4 and appliqué to the
   6½" light blocks. Add fan centers (Template 2).
3. Following quilt piecing guide on opposite page, piece
   blocks into rows, then join rows. Sew borders to
   sides, then to top and bottom.
4. Pin, baste, quilt, and bind, following directions on
   pages 14–16.

Note: Try interfaced appliqué. Machine stitch 4
fan segments together. Use pieced fan as a pattern to cut a piece of lightweight interfacing to
match. Stitch with right sides together along
outer curved edge. Turn and press, then stitch to
background with invisible thread. Interface fan
centers the same way.

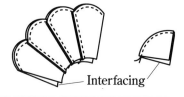

Interfacing

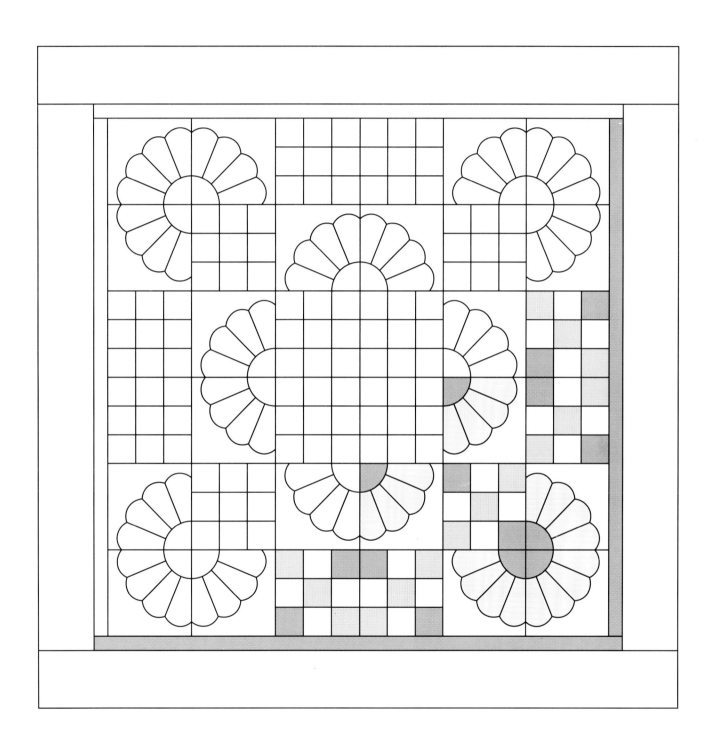

LINKED TOGETHER

Color Photo: page 27
Quilt Size: 60" x 60"
Block Size: 6"

Block A   **Block B**   **Block C**   **Block D**

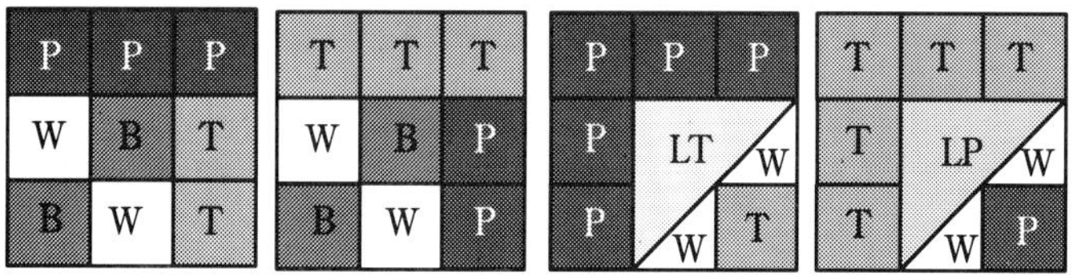

Make 16   Make 16   Make 16   Make 16

Materials: (44"-wide fabric)
1 yd. various purples (P)
1 yd. various turquoises (T)
¼ yd. light turquoise (LT)
¼ yd. light purple (LP)
⅝ yd. white (W)
⅓ yd. blue (B)
¼ yd. inner border
1 yd. outer border
3½ yds. backing
1 yd. binding
64" x 64" quilt batting

CUTTING: All strips are cut cross grain.

From the various purples, cut:
11 strips, each 2½" wide. Cut l strip into 16 squares, each 2½" x 2½".

From the various turquoises, cut:
11 strips, each 2½" wide. Cut 1 strip into 16 squares, each 2½" x 2½".

From the light turquoise, cut:
1 strip, 4⅞" wide. Cut 8 squares, each 4⅞" x 4⅞", then cut once diagonally to make 16 triangles.

From the light purple, cut:
1 strip, 4⅞" wide. Cut 8 squares, each 4⅞" x 4⅞", then cut once diagonally to make 16 triangles.

From the white, cut:
4 strips, each 2½"wide;
2 strips, each 2⅞" wide. Cut into 32 squares, each 2⅞" x 2⅞", then cut once diagonally to make 64 triangles.

From the blue, cut:
4 strips, each 2½" wide.

From the inner border fabric, cut:
5 strips, each 1½" wide. Join short ends to make one long strip, then cut 2 pieces, each 48½" long, for side borders and 2 pieces, each 50½" long, for top and bottom borders.

From the outer border fabric, cut:
6 strips, each 5½" wide. Join short ends to make one long strip, then cut 2 pieces, each 50½" long, for side borders and 2 pieces, each 60½" long, for top and bottom borders.

DIRECTIONS

1. Block A: Make 16 blocks. Use 2½"-wide strips. Following directions for Ninepatch block construction on page 10, sew:
   □ 1 set purple/purple/purple, then cut 16 segments, each 2½" wide;
   □ 1 set white/blue/turquoise, then cut 16 segments, each 2½" wide;
   □ 1 set blue/white/turquoise, then cut 16 segments, each 2½" wide. Piece into Ninepatch blocks.
2. Block B: Make 16 blocks. Use 2½"-wide strips. Following directions for Ninepatch block construction on page 10, sew:
   □ 1 set turquoise/turquoise/turquoise, then cut 16 segments, each 2½" wide;
   □ 1 set white/blue/purple, then cut 16 segments, each 2½" wide;
   □ 1 set blue/white/purple, then cut 16 segments, each 2½" wide.
   Piece into Ninepatch blocks.
3. Block C: Make 16 blocks. Use 2½"-wide strips. Sew:
   □ 1 set purple/purple/purple, then cut 16 segments, each 2½" wide;
   □ 1 set purple/purple, then cut into 16 segments, each 2½" wide.

Piece block together as shown below, using these strips, plus light turquoise and white triangles, and turquoise squares.

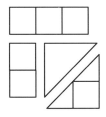

Piecing diagram for
Blocks C and D

4. Block D: Make 16 blocks. Use 2½"-wide strips. Sew:
   □ 1 set turquoise/turquoise/turquoise, then cut 16 segments, each 2½" wide;
   □ 1 set turquoise/turquoise, then cut 16 segments, each 2½" wide.
   Piece block as shown in diagram to the left, using these strips, plus light purple and white triangles, and purple squares.
5. Carefully following quilt piecing guide below, piece blocks into rows. Sew borders to sides, then to top and bottom.
6. Pin, baste, quilt, and bind, following directions on pages 14–16.

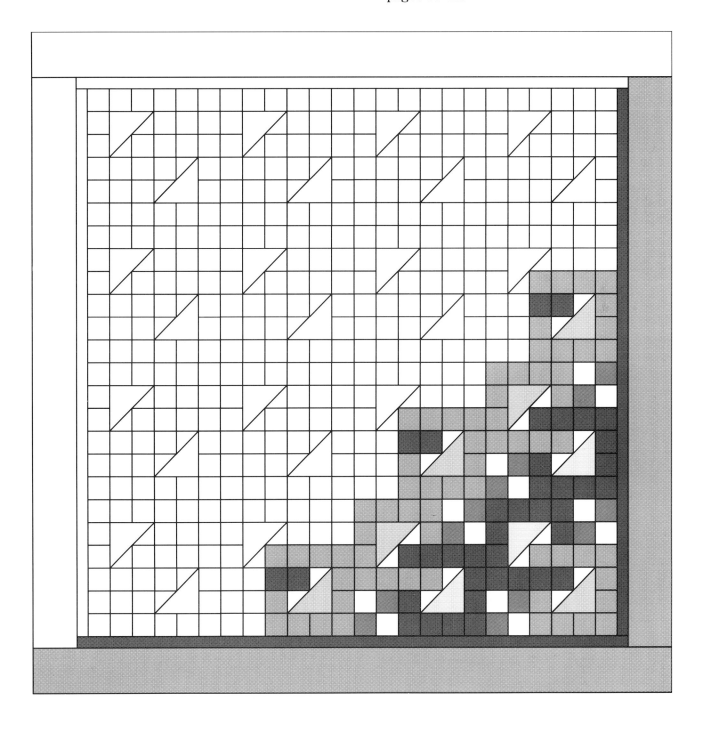

ETERNAL CHAIN

Color Photo: page 18
Quilt Size: 75" x 90"
Block Sizes: 6" and 2"

Materials: (44"-wide fabric)
4¼ yds. light (L)
1 yd. various medium greens (M)
1½ yds. various dark greens (D)
½ yd. inner border
1 yd. outer border
5½ yds. backing
1 yd. binding
79" x 94" quilt batting

Block A
L	M	L
M	L	M
L	M	L

Make 32

Block B
D	L	D
L	D	L
D	L	D

Make 31

Block C
| D | L |
| L | D |

Make 80

Block D
| M | L | M |
| L | M | L |

Make 14

Block E
| D | L | D |
| L | D | L |

Make 18

Block F
| M | L |
| L | M |

Make 4

CUTTING: All strips are cut cross grain.

From the light, cut:
28 strips, each 2½" wide;
6 strips, each 1½" wide;
9 strips, each 6½" wide. Cut 142 segments, each 2½" wide;
3 strips, each 4½" wide. Cut 36 segments, each 2½" wide.

From the medium greens, cut:
12 strips, each 2½" wide.

From the dark greens, cut:
16 strips, each 2½"wide;
6 strips, each 1½" wide.

From the inner border fabric, cut:
8 strips, each 1½" wide. Join short ends to make one long strip, then cut 2 pieces, each 82½" long, for side borders and 2 pieces, each 68½" long, for top and bottom borders.

From the outer border fabric, cut:
8 strips, each 3½" wide. Join short ends to make one long strip, then cut 2 pieces, each 84½" long, for side borders and 2 pieces, each 74½" long, for top and bottom borders.

DIRECTIONS

1. Block A: Make 32 blocks. Use 2½"-wide strips. Following directions for Ninepatch block construction on page 10, sew:
   □ 4 sets of light/medium/light, then cut 64 segments, each 2½" wide;
   □ 2 sets of medium/light/medium, then cut 32 segments, each 2½" wide.
   Piece into Ninepatch blocks.
2. Block B: Make 31 blocks. Use 2½"-wide strips. Following directions for Ninepatch block construction on page 10, sew:
   □ 4 sets dark/light/dark, then cut 62 segments, each 2½" wide;
   □ 2 sets light/dark/light, then cut 31 segments, each 2½" wide.
   Piece into Ninepatch blocks.
3. Block C: Make 80 blocks. Use 1½"-wide strips. Following directions for Four Patch construction on page 11, sew:
   □ 6 sets of dark/light, then cut 160 segments, each 1½" wide.
   Piece into Four Patch blocks.
4. Block D: Make 14 blocks. Use 2½"-wide strips. Sew:
   □ 1 set medium/light/medium, then cut 14 segments, each 2½" wide;
   □ 1 set, light/medium/light, then cut 14 segments, each 2½" wide.
   Following diagram above, piece segments into blocks that are each ⅔ of a Ninepatch block.

5. Block E: Make 18 blocks. Use 2½"-wide strips. Sew:
□ 2 sets of dark/light/dark, then cut 18 segments, each 2½" wide;
□ 2 sets light/dark/light, then cut 18 segments, each 2½" wide.
   Following diagram on page 56, piece segments into blocks that are each ⅔ of a Ninepatch block.
6. Block F: Make 4 blocks. Use 2½"-wide strips. Following directions for Four Patch construction on page 11, sew:
□ 1 set medium/light, then cut 8 segments, each 2½" wide.
   Piece into Four Patch blocks.
7. Carefully following quilt piecing guide below, piece all blocks into rows. Sew Four Patch Blocks C and F to the light background strips. Join rows of blocks with background/Four Patch strips in between rows.

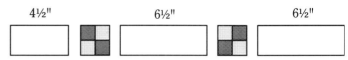

4½"   6½"   6½"

Sew borders to sides, then to top and bottom.

8. Pin, baste, quilt, and bind, following directions on pages 14–16.

Note: This quilt design relies on careful piecing of high-contrast colors to maintain a planned look, even though it is composed of a variety of different fabrics in dark and medium tones of the same color.

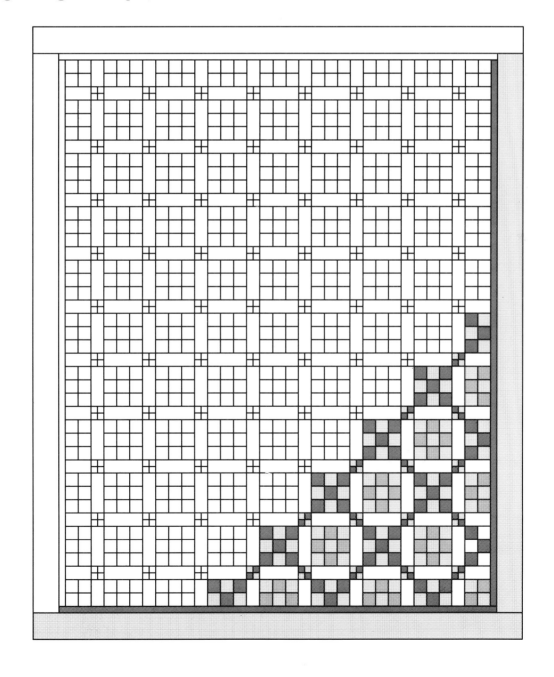

HEARTS APLENTY

Color Photo: page 28
Quilt Size: 40" x 52"
Block Size: 6"
Template: page 71

Block A

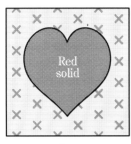

Make 18

Block B

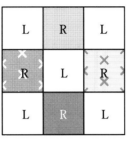

Make 17

Materials: (44"-wide fabric)
1 yd. light (L)
18 pieces, each 7" x 15", of various
   red prints (R)
¼ yd. red solid
⅔ yd. outer border
1½ yds. backing
1¼ yds. ruffle
44" x 56" quilt batting

CUTTING: All strips are cut cross grain.

From the light, cut:
6 strips, each 2½" wide. Cut into 89 squares, each
   2½" x 2½";
4 strips, each 2½" wide. Cut 10 segments, each 2½" x
   10½", and 4 segments, each 2½" x 4½";
1 strip, 4" wide. Cut 7 squares, each 4" x 4", for
   hearts.

From each of the red prints, cut:
1 square, 6½" x 6½", and 4 squares, each 2½" x 2½".

From red prints, cut:
10 squares, each 2½" x 2½".

From the red solid, cut:
2 strips, each 4" wide. Cut 11 squares, each 4" x 4".

From the border fabric, cut:
5 strips, each 3½" wide. Join short ends to make one
   long strip, then cut 2 pieces, each 46½" long, for
   side borders and 2 pieces, each 40½" long, for top
   and bottom borders.

From the ruffle fabric, cut:
8 strips, each 5" wide. Join short ends into one long
   strip.

DIRECTIONS

1. Block A: Make 18 blocks. Following directions for
   paper piecing on pages 12–13 and using Hearts
   Aplenty appliqué template on page 71, cut 18 hearts
   from paper. Cut 11 red and 7 light hearts from the 4"
   squares cut earlier. Appliqué hearts to center of 6½"
   squares.
2. On a design board or large table, position appliquéd
   heart squares as shown in the piecing guide, creating a pleasing arrangement of the various prints
   used. Lay out the small light squares with the red
   print squares to form Ninepatch blocks, making
   sure the small red squares touching each heart
   block are the same print as the fabric behind the
   heart. Add the remaining pieces around the quilt
   design to form the pieced inner border, referring to
   the diagram below.

Side borders

	10½"		10½"		10½"	

Top and bottom borders

4½"		10½"		10½"		4½"

3. Piece together each of the 17 Ninepatch blocks
   (Block B) you've created with 3 squares in each of
   3 rows.
4. Following quilt piecing guide on opposite page, piece
   blocks into rows, then join rows. Sew the pieced
   borders to the sides, then to the top and bottom. Sew
   outer border to sides, then to top and bottom.

5. Join the two short ends of the ruffle strip to create a circle. Fold ruffle in half, wrong sides together. Easestitch (long machine stitches) or hand gather ruffle ¼" from raw edges. Draw up gathering stitches to fit ruffle to outside edge of quilt. Pin with raw edges matching; distribute gathers evenly. Stitch ruffle to quilt top.

6. Pin and baste layers together and quilt, following directions on pages 14–16.

7. Turn under raw edge of backing and slipstitch to ruffle along stitching line.

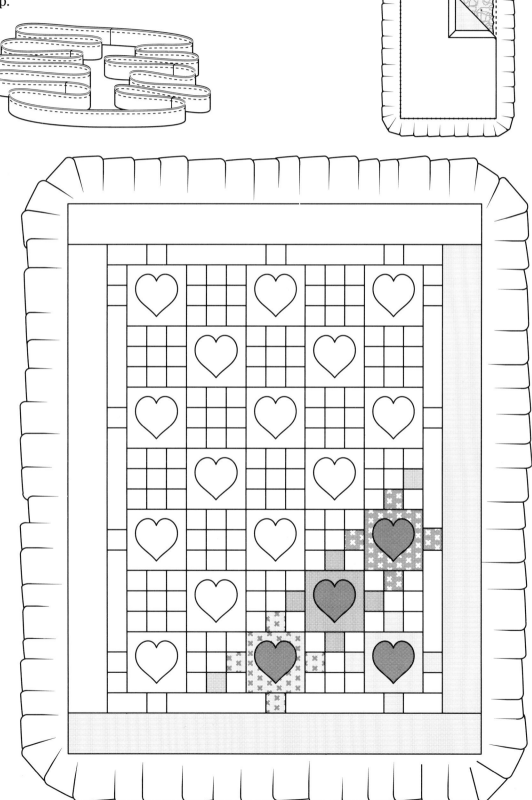

STAR SQUARE

Color Photo: page 28
Quilt Size: 48" x 60"
Block Size: 6"

Block A   **Block B**

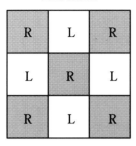 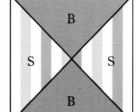

Make 32   Make 31

Materials: (44"-wide fabric)
⅔ yd. light (L)
1½ yds. red (R)
1¼ yd. blue (B)
1 yd. medium stripe (S)
3½ yds. backing
½ yd. binding
52" x 64" quilt batting

CUTTING: All strips are cut cross grain.

From the light, cut:
8 strips, each 2½" wide.

From the red, cut:
10 strips, each 2½" wide;
5 strips, each 3½" wide. From these strips, cut 14 trapezoids with long edges measuring 13¼". See Trapezoids, pages 11–12;
2 squares, each 7" x 7", then cut once diagonally to make 4 triangles.

From the blue, cut:
8 strips, each 3⅝" wide. Cut 62 triangles. See Triangles Cut from Strips, page 12;
1 strip, 7¼" wide. Cut 5 squares, each 7¼" x 7¼", then cut twice diagonally to make 18 triangles.

From the medium stripe, cut:
8 strips, each 3⅝" wide. Cut 62 triangles. See Triangles Cut from Strips, page 12.

DIRECTIONS

1. Block A: Make 32 blocks. Use 2½"-wide strips. Following directions for Ninepatch block construction on page 10, sew:
   □ 4 sets red/light/red, then cut 64 segments, each 2½" wide;
   □ 2 sets light/red/light, then cut 32 segments, each 2½" wide.
   Piece into Ninepatch blocks.
2. Block B: Make 31 blocks. Sew together as shown in block diagram.
3. Following quilt piecing guide on opposite page, piece blocks into rows, then join rows. For top and bottom pieced borders, alternate and join 4 blue triangles and 3 red trapezoids. For side borders, join 5 blue triangles and 4 red trapezoids. Sew borders to sides, then to top and bottom. Add corner triangles.
4. Pin, baste, quilt, and bind, following directions on pages 14–16.

Note: Accept the challenge of stripes! Careful cutting and piecing of the quarter-square triangle blocks is a necessity.

ARBOR ROSE

Color Photo: page 23
Quilt Size: 50" x 50"
Block Size: 6"

Block A   **Block B**

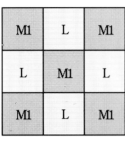 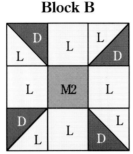

Make 25   Make 24

Materials: (44"-wide fabric)
1⅔ yds. light (L)
1 yd. first medium (M1)
¼ yd. second medium (M2)
½ yd. dark (D)
¼ yd. inner border
⅔ yd. outer border
3 yds. backing
½ yd. binding
54" x 54" quilt batting

CUTTING: All strips are cut cross grain.

From the light, cut:
15 strips, each 2½" wide. Cut 3 strips into 48 squares, each 2½" x 2½";
4 strips, each 2⅞" wide. Cut into 48 squares, each 2⅞" x 2⅞".

From the first medium, cut:
10 strips, each 2½"wide.

From the second medium, cut:
2 strips, each 2½" wide.

From the dark, cut:
4 strips, each 2⅞" wide. Cut into 48 squares, each 2⅞" x 2⅞".

From the inner border fabric, cut:
5 strips, each 1½" wide. Join short ends to make one long strip, then cut 2 pieces, each 42½" long, for side borders and 2 pieces, each 44½" long, for top and bottom borders.

From the outer border fabric, cut:
5 strips, each 3½" wide. Join short ends to make one long strip, then cut 2 pieces, each 44½" long, for side borders and 2 pieces, each 50½" long, for top and bottom borders.

DIRECTIONS

1. Sew Block A: Make 25 blocks. Use 2½"-wide strips. Following directions for Ninepatch block construction on page 10, sew:
   □ 4 sets first medium/light/first medium, then cut 50 segments, each 2½" wide;
   □ 2 sets light/first medium/light, then cut 25 segments, each 2½" wide.
   Piece into Ninepatch blocks.
2. Block B: Make 24 blocks. Sew:
   □ 2 sets light/second medium/light, then cut 24 segments, each 2½" wide.
   Pair 48 light and dark 2⅞" squares together. Following directions for half-square triangles on page 11, make 96 half-square triangles. Sew 48 strips, each composed of 2 half-square triangle units with a light square between for top and bottom of block. Sew strips into blocks, referring to Block B diagram above.

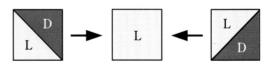

3. Following quilt piecing guide on opposite page, piece blocks into rows, then join rows. Sew borders to sides, then to top and bottom.
4. Pin, baste, quilt, and bind, following directions on pages 14–16.

Note: Precise piecing is essential to make this contrasting design stand out.

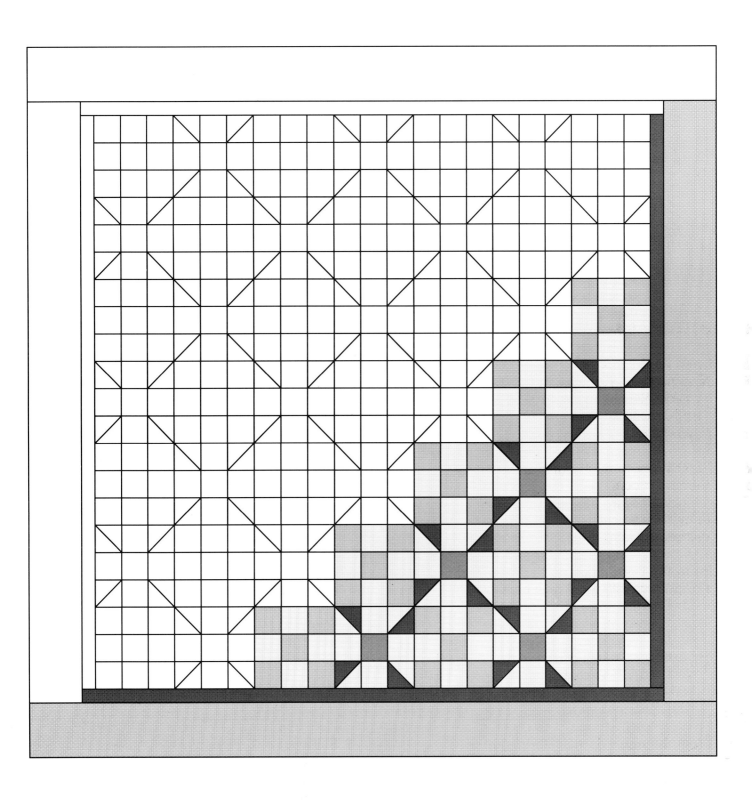

STACKED TILES

Color Photo: page 25
Quilt Size: 53" x 69½"
Block size: 6"

Materials: (44"-wide fabric)
1⅔ yds. large floral print (F)
1 yd. light (L)
1 yd. pink (P)
1¼ yds. orchid (O)
⅓ yd. violet (V)
3½ yds. backing
1 yd. binding
57" x 73" quilt batting

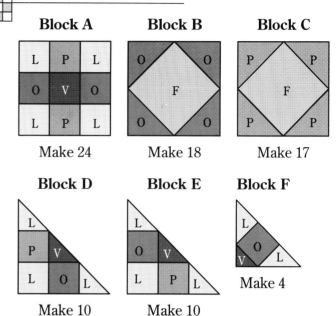

Block A — Make 24
Block B — Make 18
Block C — Make 17
Block D — Make 10
Block E — Make 10
Block F — Make 4

CUTTING: All strips are cut cross grain.

From the large floral print, cut:
5 strips, each 4¾" wide. Cut into 35 squares, each 4¾" x 4¾";
6 strips, each 4½" wide. Join short ends to make one long strip, then cut 2 pieces, each 62" long, for side borders and 2 pieces, each 53½" long, for top and bottom borders (outer border).

From the light, cut:
8 strips, each 2½" wide;
2 strips, each 4" wide. Cut into 12 squares, each 4" x 4", then cut twice diagonally to make 48 triangles.

From the pink, cut:
4 strips, each 3⅞" wide. Cut into 34 squares, each 3⅞" x 3⅞", then cut once diagonally to make 68 triangles;
5 strips, each 2½" wide.

From the orchid, cut:
4 strips, each 3⅞" wide. Cut into 36 squares, each 3⅞" x 3⅞", then cut once diagonally to make 72 triangles;
6 strips, each 2½" wide. Cut 2 strips into 24 squares, each 2½" x 2½";
5 strips, each 1½" wide. Join short ends to make one long strip, then cut 2 pieces, each 60" long, for side borders and 2 pieces, each 45½" long, for top and bottom borders (inner border).

From the violet, cut:
1 strip, 4" wide. Cut 5 squares, each 4" x 4", then cut twice diagonally to make 20 triangles;
2 strips, each 2½" wide;
2 squares, each 2½" x 2½", then cut once diagonally to make 4 triangles.

DIRECTIONS

1. Block A: Make 24 blocks. Use 2½"-wide strips. Following directions for Ninepatch block construction on page 10, sew:
☐ 3 sets light/pink/light, then cut 48 segments, each 2½" wide;
☐ 2 sets orchid/violet/orchid, then cut 24 segments, each 2½" wide.
Piece into Ninepatch blocks.
2. Block B: Make 18 blocks. Following diagram above, sew orchid triangles to sides of 18 of the floral print squares.
3. Block C: Make 17 blocks. Following diagram above, sew pink triangles to sides of the remaining 17 floral print squares.
4. Block D: Make 10 blocks. Sew:
☐ 2 sets pink/light, then cut 20 segments, each 2½" wide.

Using these segments and following diagram on opposite page, piece blocks, reserving 10 segments for step 5.

5. Block E: Make 10 blocks. Using segments from step 4 and following diagram on opposite page, piece blocks.

6. Block F: Make 4 blocks. Using remaining pieces and following diagram on opposite page, piece blocks.

7. Following quilt piecing guide below, sew blocks into diagonal rows indicated, then sew rows together. Add borders to sides, then to top and bottom.

8. Pin, baste, quilt, and bind, following directions on pages 14–16.

Note: When two lines of color in a design cross each other, the resulting color is a blend of the two separate colors. This is called transparency. In this quilt, transparency occurs when the pink and orchid lines cross and violet is the result. Experiment with your colors to achieve this added touch in your quilt.

MORNING DEW

Color Photo: page 32
Quilt Size: 57" x 70"
Block Size: 8"

Star Block

Make 20

Materials: (44"-wide fabric)
2⅔ yds. brightly colored background
1¼ yds. white (W)
20 pieces, each 4" x 9", of various colors for stars (S)
1 yd. various bright scraps (V)
4 yds. backing
1 yd. binding
61" x 74" quilt batting

CUTTING: All strips are cut cross grain.

From the background fabric, cut:
3 strips, each 8½" wide. Cut into 12 squares, each 8½" x 8½";
2 strips, each 12½" wide. Cut 4 squares, each 12½ x 12½", then cut twice diagonally to make 14 setting triangles. From remaining strip, cut 2 squares, each 9" x 9", then cut once diagonally to make 4 corner triangles;
6 strips, each 6" wide. Join short ends to make one long strip, then cut 2 pieces, each 56½" long, for side borders and 2 pieces, each 58" long, for top and bottom borders.

From the white, cut:
7 strips, each 2½" wide. Cut 80 segments, each 3½" wide;
15 strips, each 1½" wide.

From the star fabrics, cut:
1 square, 2½" x 2½", for each star;
8 squares, each 1½" x 1½", for each star.

From the bright scraps, cut:
12 strips, each 1½" wide, or 24 strips, each 1½" x 22" (half width of fabric).

DIRECTIONS

1. Make 80 Ninepatch blocks. Use 1½"-wide strips. Following directions for Ninepatch block construction on page 10, sew:
   □ 6 sets white/scrap/white, then cut 160 segments, each 1½"wide;
   □ 3 sets scrap/white/scrap, then cut 80 segments, each 1½" wide.
   Piece into Ninepatch blocks.

> **Note:** If using 1½" x 22" strips, sew 12 sets white/scrap/white and 6 sets scrap/white/scrap.

2. Star Block: Make 20 blocks. Following directions for quick-geese block construction on page 12, sew 2 squares, each 1½" x 1½", to short side of each white 3½" segment.

3. Piece blocks together, following diagram.

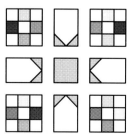

4. Following quilt piecing guide below, sew Star blocks, Ninepatch blocks, and setting triangles in diagonal rows.
5. Add borders to sides, then to top and bottom.
6. Pin, baste, quilt, and bind, following directions on pages 14–16.

Note: The random piecing in the tiny Double Ninepatch blocks is worth the extra time spent to make this cheery quilt.

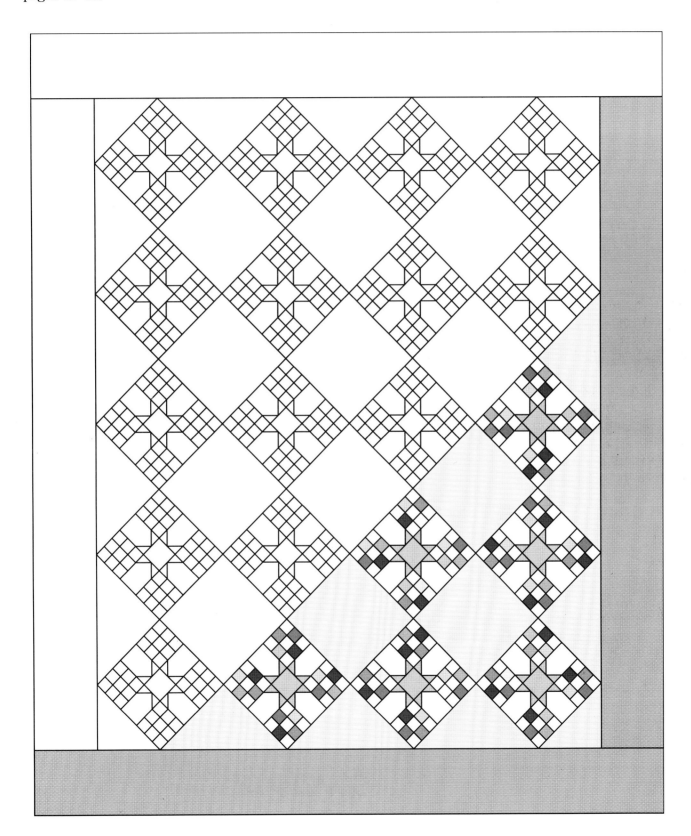

STEP BY STEP

Color Photo: page 21
Quilt Size: 68" x 68"
Block size: 9"

Block A   **Block B**   **Block C**

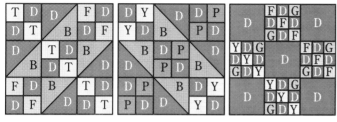

Make 12   Make 8   Make 16

Materials: (44"-wide fabric)
2½ yds. dark (D)
¼ yd. purple (P)
½ yd. yellow (Y)
½ yd. fuchsia (F)
½ yd. blue (B)
¼ yd. turquoise (T)
⅓ yd. green (G)
⅓ yd. inner border
1½ yds. outer border
4 yds. backing
1 yd. binding
72" x 72" quilt batting

CUTTING: All strips are cut cross grain.

From the dark, cut:
4 strips, each 3⅞" wide. Cut into 40 squares, each
    3⅞" x 3⅞";
12 strips, each 2" wide;
14 strips, each 1½" wide;
7 strips, each 3½" wide. Cut into 80 squares, each
    3½" x 3½".

From the purple, cut:
3 strips, each 2" wide.

From the yellow, cut:
2 strips, each 2" wide;
5 strips, each 1½" wide.

From the fuchsia, cut:
3 strips, each 2" wide;
5 strips, each 1½" wide.

From the blue, cut:
4 strips, each 3⅞" wide. Cut into 40 squares, each
    3⅞" x 3⅞".

From the turquoise, cut:
4 strips, each 2" wide.

From the green, cut:
6 strips, each 1½" wide.

From the inner border fabric, cut:
6 strips, each 1½" wide. Join short ends to make one
    long strip, then cut 2 pieces, each 54½" long, for
    side borders and 2 pieces, each 56½" long, for top
    and bottom borders.

From the outer border fabric, cut:
7 strips, each 6½" wide. Join short ends to make one
    long strip, then cut 2 pieces, each 56½" long, for
    side borders and 2 pieces, each 68½" long, for top
    and bottom borders.

DIRECTIONS

1. Block A: Make 12 blocks. Use 2"-wide and 3⅞"-wide
   strips. Following directions for half-square triangles
   on page 11, pair 40 dark and 40 blue 3⅞" squares
   with right sides together. Use 48 of these in Block A
   and the remaining 32 in Block B.

Following directions for Four Patch block construction on page 11 and using 2"-wide strips, sew:
☐ 3 sets dark/fuchsia, then cut 48 segments, each 2"
   wide. Piece 24 Four Patch units.
☐ 4 sets dark/turquoise, then cut 72 segments, each 2"
   wide. Piece 36 Four Patch units.

Following diagram on opposite page, piece 5 Four Patch units and 4 half-square triangle units into Block A.

2. Block B: Make 8 blocks. Use 32 half-square triangle units from step 1 and 2"-wide strips. Sew:

☐ 3 sets dark/purple, then cut 48 segments, each 2" wide. Sew 24 Four Patch units.

☐ 2 sets dark/yellow, then cut 32 segments, each 2" wide. Sew 16 Four Patch units.

Following diagram on opposite page, piece Four Patch units and half-square triangles, set aside from step 1, into Block B.

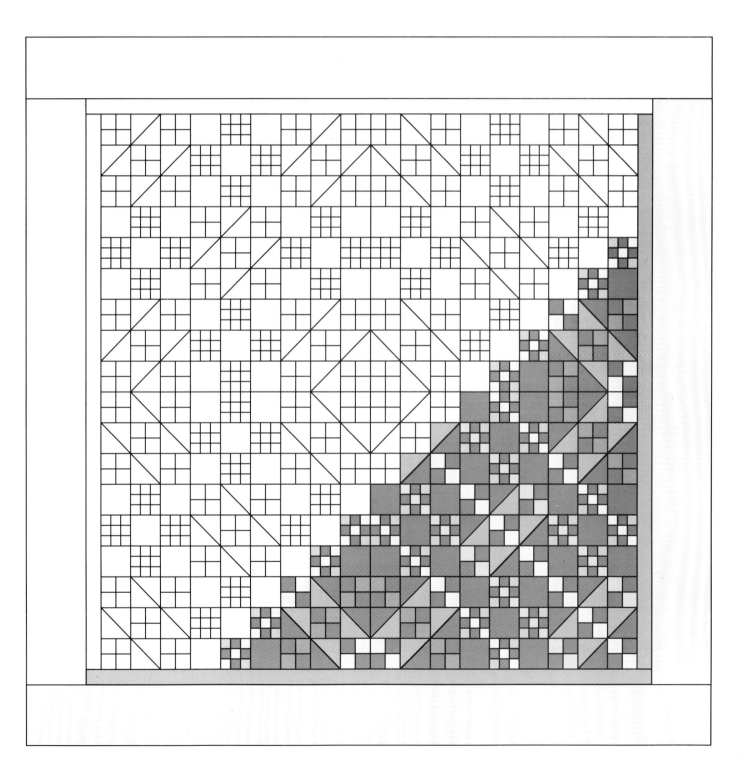

3. Block C: Make 16 blocks. Use 1½"-wide strips. Sew:
- [ ] 3 sets fuchsia/dark/green, then cut 64 segments, each 1½" wide;
- [ ] 2 sets dark/fuchsia/dark, then cut 32 segments, each 1½" wide.

Following diagram below, piece into Ninepatch blocks.

- [ ] 3 sets yellow/dark/green, then cut 64 segments, each 1½" wide;
- [ ] 2 sets dark/yellow/dark, then cut 32 segments, each 1½" wide.

Following diagram below, piece into Ninepatch blocks.

Using 3½" dark squares and the 2 sets of different Ninepatch blocks just made, piece together into Block C as shown on page 68.

> **Note:** Be sure to play with these blocks before sewing them together. There are many designs waiting to make their debut.

4. Following quilt piecing guide on page 69, piece blocks into rows, then join rows. Add side borders, then top and bottom borders.
5. Pin, baste, quilt, and bind, following directions on pages 14–16.

> **Note:** When cutting Four Patch segments, stack 2 strips of opposite colors, right sides together, and cut in pairs. This method positions segments in correct sequence for stitching, to complete the Four Patch block.

TEMPLATES

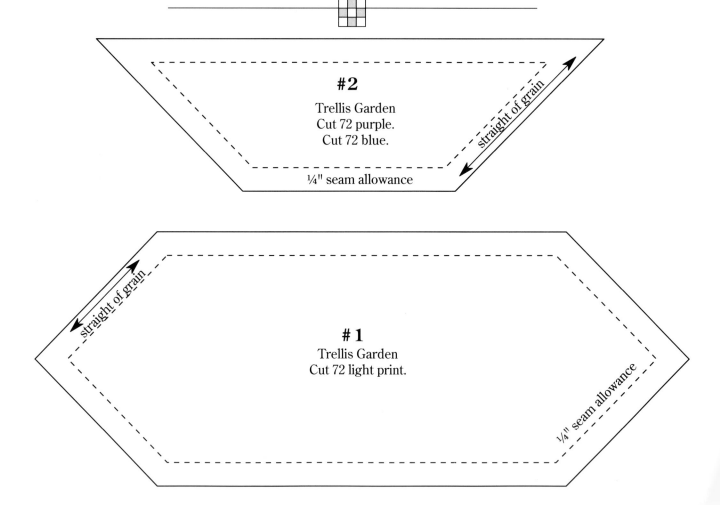

#2

Trellis Garden
Cut 72 purple.
Cut 72 blue.

straight of grain

¼" seam allowance

#1

Trellis Garden
Cut 72 light print.

straight of grain

¼" seam allowance

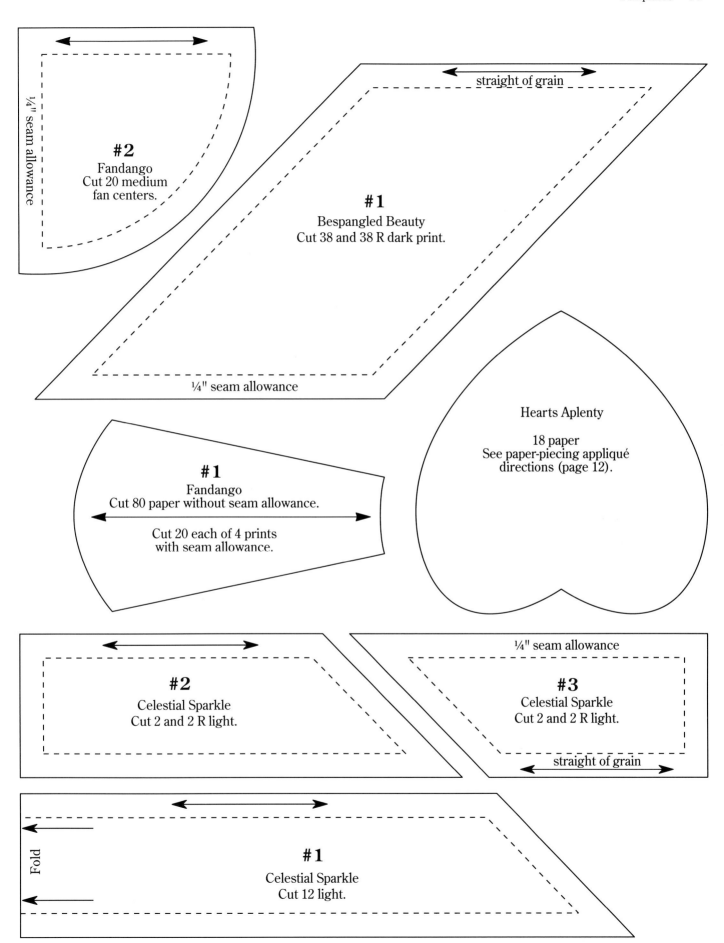

#2
Fandango
Cut 20 medium
fan centers.

¼" seam allowance

#1
Bespangled Beauty
Cut 38 and 38 R dark print.

straight of grain

¼" seam allowance

Hearts Aplenty

18 paper
See paper-piecing appliqué
directions (page 12).

#1
Fandango
Cut 80 paper without seam allowance.

Cut 20 each of 4 prints
with seam allowance.

#2
Celestial Sparkle
Cut 2 and 2 R light.

¼" seam allowance

#3
Celestial Sparkle
Cut 2 and 2 R light.

straight of grain

Fold

#1
Celestial Sparkle
Cut 12 light.

That Patchwork Place Publications and Products

BOOKS

Angelsong by Joan Vibert
Angle Antics by Mary Hickey
Appliqué Borders: An Added Grace by Jeana Kimball
Back to Square One by Nancy J. Martin
Baltimore Bouquets by Mimi Dietrich
A Banner Year by Nancy J. Martin
Basket Garden by Mary Hickey
Blockbuster Quilts by Margaret J. Miller
Calendar Quilts by Joan Hanson
Cathedral Window: A Fresh Look by Nancy J. Martin
Copy Art for Quilters by Nancy J. Martin
Corners in the Cabin by Paulette Peters
Country Threads by Connie Tesene and Mary Tendall
Even More by Trudie Hughes
Fantasy Flowers: Pieced Flowers for Quilters
    by Doreen Cronkite Burbank
Feathered Star Sampler by Marsha McCloskey
Fit To Be Tied by Judy Hopkins
Five- and Seven-Patch Blocks & Quilts for the ScrapSaver™
    by Judy Hopkins
Four-Patch Blocks & Quilts for the ScrapSaver
    by Judy Hopkins
Handmade Quilts by Mimi Dietrich
Happy Endings—Finishing the Edges of Your Quilt
    by Mimi Dietrich
Holiday Happenings by Christal Carter
Home for Christmas by Nancy J. Martin and Sharon Stanley
In The Beginning by Sharon Evans Yenter
Jacket Jazz by Judy Murrah
Lessons in Machine Piecing by Marsha McCloskey
Little By Little: Quilts in Miniature by Mary Hickey
Loving Stitches: A Guide to Fine Hand Quilting
    by Jeana Kimball
More Template-Free™ *Quiltmaking* by Trudie Hughes
My Mother's Quilts: Designs from the Thirties
    by Sara Nephew
Nifty Ninepatches by Carolann M. Palmer
Nine-Patch Blocks & Quilts for the ScrapSaver™
    by Judy Hopkins
Not Just Quilts by Jo Parrott
Ocean Waves by Marsha McCloskey and Nancy J. Martin
One-of-a-Kind Quilts by Judy Hopkins
On to Square Two by Marsha McCloskey
Osage County Quilt Factory by Virginia Robertson
Painless Borders by Sally Schneider
A Perfect Match: A Guide to Precise Machine Piecing
    by Donna Lynn Thomas

Picture Perfect Patchwork by Naomi Norman
Pineapple Passion by Nancy Smith and Lynda Milligan
A Pioneer Doll and Her Quilts by Mary Hickey
Pioneer Storybook Quilts by Mary Hickey
*Quick & Easy Quiltmaking: 26 Projects Featuring Speedy
    Cutting and Piecing Methods* by Mary Hickey,
    Nancy J. Martin, Marsha McCloskey & Sara Nephew
Quilts for All Seasons: Year-Round Log Cabin Designs
    by Christal Carter
Quilts from Nature by Joan Colvin
Quilts to Share by Janet Kime
Red and Green: An Appliqué Tradition by Jeana Kimball
Red Wagon Originals by Gerry Kimmel and Linda Brannock
Reflections of Baltimore by Jeana Kimball
Rotary Riot: 40 Fast and Fabulous Quilts by Judy Hopkins
    and Nancy J. Martin
Scrap Happy by Sally Schneider
*Sensational Settings: Over 80 Ways to Arrange Your Quilt
    Blocks* by Joan Hanson
Shortcuts: A Concise Guide to Metric Rotary Cutting
    by Donna Lynn Thomas
Shortcuts: A Concise Guide to Rotary Cutting
    by Donna Lynn Thomas
Small Talk by Donna Lynn Thomas
Smoothstitch™ *Quilts: Easy Machine Appliqué*
    by Roxi Eppler
Stars and Stepping Stones by Marsha McCloskey
Strips That Sizzle by Margaret J. Miller
Tea Party Time: Romantic Quilts and Tasty Tidbits
    by Nancy J. Martin
Template-Free™ *Quiltmaking* by Trudie Hughes
Template-Free™ *Quilts and Borders* by Trudie Hughes
Threads of Time by Nancy J. Martin
Women and Their Quilts by Nancyann Johanson Twelker

TOOLS

6" Bias Square®
8" Bias Square®
Metric Bias Square®
BiRangle™
Pineapple Rule
Rotary Mate™
Rotary Rule™
ScrapSaver™

VIDEO

Shortcuts to America's
Best-Loved Quilts

That Patchwork Place®

Many titles are available at your local quilt shop. For more information, send $2 for a color catalog to That Patchwork Place, Inc., PO Box 118, Bothell WA 98041-0118 USA.

☎ Call 1-800-426-3126 for the name and location of the quilt shop nearest you.